EDUCATION FOR MINISTRY

FRONT ENTRANCE

Education for Ministry

BRISTOL BAPTIST COLLEGE
1679 - 1979

By

NORMAN S. MOON, B.A., B.D., M.Th.

Senior Tutor and Librarian,
Bristol Baptist College

Foreword by

The Reverend David S. Russell, M.A., B.D., D.Litt.

General Secretary, The Baptist Union of Great Britain
and Ireland

BRISTOL BAPTIST COLLEGE
WOODLAND ROAD
BRISTOL

ISBN 0 906622 00 X

Made and printed in Great Britain by
Stanley L. Hunt (Printers) Ltd.,
Rushden, Northamptonshire

Foreword

There is a justifiable note of pride in the pages of this book, for Bristol Baptist College has a great history and, after 300 years of outstanding service, is very much alive at this present time, enabling a new generation of students to understand the Christian Gospel for themselves and to interpret it in a way that matches the pressing needs of this hour.

The College is to be congratulated on attaining its Tercentenary; and the author of this commemorative book, the Rev. Norman Moon, is to be congratulated also on the completion of a meticulous record that demonstrates quite clearly the great contribution made in the field of theological education by this the oldest of all the Baptist Colleges.

There is an old Chinese proverb which says, 'If you are planning for a year, plant seed; if you are planning for a generation, plant trees; if you are planning for generations to come, plant men.' Bristol Baptist College obviously believes in long-term investment. From the beginning it has invested in men – and women – and has counted such expenditure in time, effort and money well spent. The reader of these pages cannot but be deeply impressed by the number and quality of outstanding leaders it has produced over the years – men and women who are household names among Baptists, some of whom indeed have received national and even international acclaim. This slim volume is of much more than domestic interest; it is in its own way a social history of the past 300 years as seen through the eyes of Baptist Non-conformists, amply illustrated by vivid pen portraits of succeeding generations of students. The College has helped to train ministers of the Gospel from many parts of the world and today its influence is felt not only in Britain and in the New World, but also in the Orient and in the Socialist countries of Eastern Europe.

This short history makes manifestly clear that Bristol Baptist College believes in an educated and cultured ministry as well as in a devout and dedicated ministry. Holding pride of place in its curriculum is the study of theology and its related subjects. But its aim is not so much to give instruction in theology as an academic discipline as it is to help its students to understand the better the nature and the activity of God in this world he has made. For this reason the curriculum from early days was broadly based, embracing not only theology, but English literature, Biblical languages, Logic, Philosophy and Science as well. For the same reason the students of today have not only to 'study' theology, but also to 'do' theology, seeing it in relation to the insights and trends of other academic disciplines and the social and pastoral problems of a multi-cultural society. Such a curriculum takes academic study seriously; but it is a 'practical' discipline which is rooted in the activity of God in the life of present-day society and in the lives of ordinary people.

Its objective is to train men and women of God who are open to the spirit of truth in whatever form it may appear. Its tradition has been and remains that of spiritual and mental integrity, testing the spirits to see whether they are of God (cf. 1 John 4.1). And its prayer is:

> 'From the cowardice that dare not face new truth;
> From the laziness that is contented with half-truths;
> And from the arrogance that imagines it knows all truth –
> Good Lord, deliver us.'

Again and again, and not least at this present time, the College has shown vision, imagination and courage in shaping and re-shaping its programme to meet the needs of the Church and the Gospel in contemporary society. Those who know the present Principal and tutors and the members of the College Committee look with confidence to the future, assured that this worthy tradition stretching over 300 years will not only be maintained but also enhanced in the providence of God.

D. S. RUSSELL, *General Secretary,*
Baptist Union of Great Britain and Ireland.

December, 1978

Preface

This book has been written for the Tercentenary celebrations of Bristol Baptist College. The College owes its foundation to the deed of gift made by Edward Terrill to Broadmead Baptist Church dated 3rd June 1679. It is the oldest Baptist College in the world and the oldest surviving Free Church College in this country.

The primary aim of the book is to relate the history of the College through three centuries, to describe its life and enduring purpose, that of preparing able and evangelical ministers for Baptist Churches. About 1,400 students have been educated here.

In 1884 S. A. Swaine published *Faithful Men: or, Memorials of Bristol Baptist College, and some of its most distinguished alumni,* which included biographical sketches of many of the more celebrated Bristol men. This book does not attempt to up-date Swaine, an enterprise which would require a much larger volume and involve difficulties of selection. But in order to *illustrate* something of the influence of the College over the generations, *Education for Ministry* selects – almost at random – from the careers of some of the former students. Many others might equally merit mention, and no lack of appreciation is implied in their omission.

A secondary purpose of this Tercentenary publication has been to document the sources of the history of the College, particularly in its earlier years in the hope that this will stimulate others to research in some particular aspects of the work of the College.

The general reader will no doubt also find points of fascinating interest in some of the detail which is included in the extensive notes. To have included this in the narrative would have made it too cumbersome.

Although this book is published by the College under the authorship of Norman Moon, it would not have been possible without the assistance of the Reverend Sidney Hall whose detailed research into the records of the College and its former students has been card-indexed with meticulous care.

My colleague, the Reverend Harry Mowvley, and the Reverend

Walter Bottoms have devoted much time to help me to prepare the manuscript for publication. They and many others have given valuable advice and encouragement as the work has proceeded.

Special gratitude is due to the Reverend Dr. Leonard Champion, the Reverend Roger Hayden, the Reverend Dr. Geoffrey Nuttall, the Reverend Dr. Ernest Payne, and the College Principal, the Reverend Dr. Morris West.

I am also grateful for the patience of Mrs. Eunice Welch and Mrs. Pearl Woolnough who have typed and re-typed the manuscript.

For most of the photography we are indebted to Mr. David Bodey, and for the charts to the Reverend Philip Webb.

NORMAN MOON.

Bristol Baptist College
January, 1979

Contents

List of Illustrations

CHAPTER ONE

Beginning the Work

1679 – 1758

1. The Birth of the Idea

On 3rd of June, 1679, Edward Terrill,[1] a wealthy Bristolian and elder of the Broadmead Baptist Church signed a deed of gift in favour of his church. It was to be used, after his death, for the support of a minister at Broadmead who was 'well skilled in the tongues' of Hebrew and Greek, and whose chief task would be that of preparing young men for ministry among the Baptist churches of the land.

Such was the modest beginning from which Bristol Baptist College has sprung. The importance of the task to which Terrill challenged his successors has continued to be recognised through three centuries. Because the money was vested in the ministry of a local church, the work has remained firmly rooted geographically in the city of its birth. Although now its legal and constitutional links with Broadmead have been severed, the College has remained closely identified with that church and with others in Bristol and the South West of England. At the same time the influence of the pioneer Baptist College in the world has spread to all quarters of the globe.

With the closure in 1977 of New College, London (which had historical links with Congregational Academies going back before 1700, and an endowment dating from 1673), Bristol Baptist College is the oldest surviving Free Church College.

When Edward Terrill set his pen to paper to make his bequest, the times were very difficult for all who could not accept the teaching and practice of the Established Church of England. Baptists, like all Dissenters, were an illegal body and were being persecuted. In the previous year, 1678, John Bunyan had published *The Pilgrim's Progress* written in Bedford gaol where he had been a prisoner for conscience' sake for many

years. Two of Broadmead's ministers had also suffered im-
prisonment for their convictions. In 1679 the Church was
anxious to find a well-qualified man to succeed Thomas
Hardcastle[2] who had recently died at the age of 42, probably
due to his privations in prison. Like many Puritan ministers of
his generation, he had enjoyed the benefits of a University
education during Cromwell's Commonwealth and Protec-
torate. When this came to an end with the restoration of the
monarchy in 1660, the doors of Oxford and Cambridge closed
against everybody who refused to conform to the Established
Church, and remained closed for nearly two hundred years.
The Puritans believed that the Minister of the Word of God
needed to be well educated, gifted in the knowledge of the
Scriptures and able to understand them in the original languages. Edward Terrill, a layman, understood to some extent
the biblical languages. He was anxious to remove any reproach
that Baptist ministers lacked proper intellectual equipment for
their ministry.

It was a tremendous act of faith for Terrill to invest in a
Dissenting ministry in this way at a time when it would have
been easy to think it had no future.

Baptists were divided about the desirability of an educated
ministry. Some believed that education – 'human learning' –
was inhibiting to the Spirit. For example, Samuel How, a
Baptist preacher in Coleman Street, London, wrote a pamphlet
with the lengthy title:

> *The Sufficiency of the Spirit's Teaching without Humane Learn-*
> *ing: or, a Treatise Tending to prove Humane Learning to be No*
> *Help to the Spiritual Understanding of the Word of God* (1639).

Thomas Collier, who was a Messenger among Baptists in the
West Country, argued in 1651 that 'it is the spirit of Antichrist
that seeks after humane help to supply the room or want of
this Spirit of Christ and having gotten it they grow proud of it,
are self conceited in it, make it their idol and dare reproach
the Spirit and power of the Lord and His saints.'

Other Baptists however thought differently.[3] In 1675 a group
of ministers in London wrote to their colleagues in the pro-
vinces, inviting them to a meeting to discuss a plan to provide
education for future ministers. It was not until 1689, after the
passing of the Act of Toleration which released Dissenters from

harassment, that such a meeting could take place. When it did, this Assembly issued a declaration appealing for a fund for three main purposes: to provide stipends so that ministers need not undertake secular work, to sponsor ministers for pioneer ministries, and to help any who were called to the ministry to study for their vocation. Among the signatories were Thomas Vaux, minister of Broadmead, and Andrew Gifford, minister of the nearby Pithay Baptist Church in Bristol.[4] The Pithay church contributed £30, and the church in Plymouth an immediate £27, to be followed by an annual subscription of £9. Plymouth's gift was to be used entirely for the education of young ministers. The Plymouth church also nominated one of their members, Richard Sampson, to be maintained and to be tutored by a certain William Thomas[5] in Bristol, but Sampson cannot legitimately be regarded as the first student of Bristol College since he was supported by this newer fund and not by the Broadmead Trust set up to administer Terrill's bequest.

Edward Terrill died about 1685, but it was not until after the death of his wife Dorothy, about 1697, that monies from his estate became available. By 1711 two other Broadmead members, Daniel Gwilliam and Robert Bodenham, had left further money for the same purpose.[6]

In 1714, a certain Caleb Jope was appointed assistant minister at Broadmead. He had studied at the Trowbridge Academy set up by John Davisson for the training of General Baptist ministers, and now he was given help from the Terrill Fund to further his studies at the Tewkesbury Academy[7] so that he might serve as assistant minister at Broadmead and act as Tutor to ministerial students. Unfortunately he proved unsuitable for the work and left for Plymouth in 1719.

2. Bernard Foskett's Ministry 1720 – 1758

So it was not until the arrival of Bernard Foskett[8] (1685-1758) in Bristol in 1720 that the vision of 1679 became a reality. Foskett had been co-pastor of the Baptist Churches at Alcester and Henley-in-Arden in Warwickshire, but now was invited to become assistant minister to Peter Kitterell at Broadmead. Since the Terrill Fund was to be used to pay his stipend, he saw his primary task as being to educate young men for the ministry. Consequently he did not regard himself as the pastor, and only presided at the Lord's Table when the minister was ill. It was not until Peter Kitterell died in 1727 that Foskett became pastor in the full sense.

There are no surviving records of the College relating to the period before 1770; some details of the story can be gathered from the Broadmead minute books. The first students, accepted in 1720, were both Welshmen: Thomas Rogers, originally from Pontypool, was a member of the Pithay Church Bristol; John Phillips came from Rhydwilym, Carmarthenshire. Each received a grant of £10 from Terrill's bequest and was helped further by two other funds which had been established in 1717, the Particular Baptist Fund and the Bristol Baptist Fund.[9] It was not until 1727 that a third student arrived – another Welshman, Daniel Garnon, from Carmarthenshire.

When Bernard Foskett became pastor at Broadmead the church decided to appoint another assistant. They invited Andrew Gifford[10] whose father, Emmanuel, was minister at the Pithay Church and whose grandfather, Andrew, had signed the 1689 declaration regarding education of ministers. Young Andrew Gifford began work at Broadmead in early 1728, but towards the end of 1729 accepted a call to the Church in Little Wild Street, London. It may be that he was disappointed that more young men were not coming forward for training. However, as later events show, he retained a very strong interest in the work in Bristol.

In 1730 a young man of eighteen, Hugh Evans,[11] came from a notable Baptist family in Wales to Bristol for medical advice on a lame foot and stayed with his aunt who was a member of Broadmead. He was already a well-educated young man, especially gifted in the ancient languages and now, during his fifteen-month stay in the city, he continued his studies under Bernard Foskett, and was baptised by him. Foskett took to him at once and recognised his potential as a minister. He wrote to Hugh's father, who was minister at Dolau and Pentre in Radnorshire, encouraging him to test the boy's gifts for ministry. Apparently he did so, for three years later Hugh returned to Bristol when the Broadmead Church gave him a call 'to preach the Gospel where Providence should call him'. Several churches at different times called him to be their pastor but he 'could by no means think of rending himself from Broadmead'. In 1739 in accordance with normal procedure, the church called Hugh Evans to the office of teaching elder, and he was ordained. By this time he had married Sarah Browne of Broadmead.

Two houses in North Street, Bristol,[12] had been given to the church for the use of its ministers, and here Foskett and Evans settled down not only to minister to the Broadmead church but also to provide education for those intending to become Baptist ministers. Though there was an age gap of 30 years between them they worked in perfect harmony for twenty-four years. As personalities they complemented each other. Foskett, who we assume remained a bachelor, was an austere man with a prodigious memory which allowed him to learn Homer in Greek, sixty lines at a time! His portrait has been described as 'revealing a man with piercing flint-like chin, and tightly closed mouth'. But he had the reputation for benevolence especially to the poor members of his flock.

Hugh Evans was a warmer personality with a characteristic Welsh vivacity – a lively preacher, who exercised a great influence on his students.

Between 1735 and 1740 about a dozen men were sent by churches, most of them in Wales and 'put under Mr. Foskett and Mr. Evans'. Such men had been tested by their home churches for their fitness for the Christian ministry, though a few came simply for education without specific commitment to the ministry. During their training they became 'transient' members of the Broadmead Church. They lived with the Principal and Tutor in the houses in North Street, sharing in meals and in prayers as members of the family.

During the 1740s, a steady stream of students came not only from Wales but also from the West Country – two came from London, two from Tottlebank in Lancashire and one even from Dublin. One of these students, John Collett Ryland,[13] who had come from Bourton-on-the-Water, kept a very revealing diary which gives an insight into the life of the students and indicates how their education was received not simply in the class-room but also in the community. He tells how 'my rapacious appetite may well make me blush', and how he was rebuked for 'unmanly conduct towards Mrs. Evans at supper'!

It apparently did him some good for he confesses in a later
entry that 'this day at dinner I happily fell into a strain of
telling remarkable stories and events, O! that I may be assisted
to provide suitable, seasonable, pleasant, profitable entertain-
ment this way whenever I've an opportunity'. It seems students
have not changed much! Foskett also helped to discipline him
in the art of prayer. 'Mr. Foskett gave me a hint today about
expressions in prayer, not to be too rash!'

Ryland's appetite at meal-times was at least matched by his
appetite for reading, and there was ample opportunity for the
feeding of the mind. Foskett himself was broadly educated. He
had studied various branches of literature and also medicine.
In his funeral tribute to him, Hugh Evans declared 'though
he spent a considerable time in qualifying himself to do good
to the bodies of men, he chose now to serve them in the important way of doing good to their souls, preferring the character
of an able minister to that of a skilful physician'; though he
still prescribed for his students and congregation when they
were ill. The breadth of Foskett's education is reflected in the
teaching given to his students.[14] He lectured on what now
would be called Philosophy of Religion and Psychology, as
well as Logic, Ethics, Music and Politics. Ryland claims that
his studies included five languages – English, Latin, Greek,
Hebrew and French – as well as Rhetoric, Logic, History and
Geography. On the more strictly theological side in 1745 he
studied parts of the Old Testament, the whole of the New
Testament which he read through three times, the Baptist
Catechism and Confession of Faith, and Christian Doctrine.

The Baptist College at Bristol needs to be seen in the context
of the wider field of education provided by the Dissenting
Academies.[15] When the Act of Uniformity (1662) excluded
Dissenters from the two English Universities, a number of
ejected ministers set up academies to provide higher education
for the sons of Dissenters. In the seventeenth century these were
private institutions, in which a suitably gifted minister gathered
around him twenty or thirty students, and prepared them for
their vocation in Law, Medicine or the Christian Ministry.
During the eighteenth century, many of those academies
became public institutions, supported by a 'society' or a group
of trustees. The range of subjects covered was wider than the

PORTRAITS OF PRINCIPALS

BERNARD FOSKETT

HUGH EVANS

CALEB EVANS

JOHN RYLAND

An account of the

Constitution of the Bristol Education Society.

1st Meeting.

Broad-mead. Vestry: Thursday 7th June 1770. 10 oclock Morning.

Present

Revd. H. Evans,	Revd. Peter Evans.	
——— Jnº Tommas,	——— Saml. Danscombe,	Mr. Joseph Mason,
——— Cº Evans,	——— Thoº. Twining,	Mr. John Page, Junr.,
——— I. Newton,	——— Danl. Sprague,	Mr Francis Parry,
——— Robt. Day,	Mr. Thoª. Parry, Senr.	Mr John Morgan,
——— John Ash,	Joseph Tomkins Esqr.	Mr Joseph Betts,
——— Benjn. Francis,	Willm. Tomkins Esqr.	Mr Willm. Clissold,
——— Thoª. Lewis,	John Bull Esqr.	Mr. Lazarus Brown.
——— John Kingdon,	Mr. Willm. Steele,	Mr. John Thomas.
		Mr. Thomas Mullett.

The above Gentn. being met, in consequence of the circular letter of invitation for that purpose. The meeting was opend in prayer by the Revd. Mr Tommas. The Society, was then constituted upon the following plan, and under the following regulations. ——————— Vizt

To the end that Dissenting Congregations, (especially of the Baptist denomination) in any part of the British Dominions, may if it please God to succeed our endeavours, be more effectually supplied with a succession of able and evangelical Ministers; We whose names are underwritten; and who have each subscribed at least one Guinea pr Ann: for the purpose above mentiond, do by these presents enter into a voluntary association under the following regulations.

1st That the Society hereby constituted be known by the name of the Bristol Education Society.

2dy That twelve subscribing Members be chosen Trustees, in whose names the capital stock of this Society shall be invested, and who shall be impowerd to place out what may be subscribed toward the said Capital, as well as what may be at any time appropriated to it, upon such security as the Society, shall approve of, and to receive the Interest of the same; for the use of the Society.

3dy That some one of the Members residing in or near the City of Bristol be chosen Treasurer to the Society, who shall be impowerd to receive the annual subscription

MINUTES OF 1770 – FIRST PAGE

narrowly classical studies of the Universities. The sciences (Medicine, Anatomy, Chemistry), Mathematics, Geography, History, Law and Theology were taught. So high was the reputation of these academies, that a number of Anglican parents preferred to send their sons there. Future lawyers, doctors, non-conformist ministers (including a few Baptists), even future bishops, shared in the provision of these progressive educational institutions. They became the forerunners of modern Universities. One of the most notable of these academies was run by the Congregational minister, Philip Doddridge, at Northampton. The curriculum of Foskett compared not unfavourably with that of Doddridge, though Bristol was a smaller community and limited its work to the educating of men for the Baptist Ministry. Many Dissenting Academies moved around, as their Principals migrated, and some changed in character. By rooting his bequest in a *church* Terrill ensured the continuity of the academy at Bristol.

It is significant that as the eighteenth century proceeded, Congregational Churches began to have second thoughts about sending their ministerial candidates to some of the academies. While they valued their academic freedom, they became increasingly uneasy about their tendency towards Unitarian doctrines. The trustees of denominational funds began to establish theological colleges devoted particularly to the training of ministers. One Congregational College, at Ottery St. Mary in Devon, was founded in 1752, later moved first to Plymouth and then to Bristol, and became Western College, a College destined to have close relations with the Bristol Baptist College.[16]

Altogether some 64 men studied under Foskett over a period of 30 years for the latter part of which he was joined by Hugh Evans.[17] John Rippon in his *Essay towards a History of the Baptist Academy at Bristol* (1795), claims that while Foskett was not the 'first of tutors' since he was 'severe, rather than enchanting; employing the memory more than the genius, the reasoning more than the softer powers of the mind', he is eager to acknowledge that 'several of the greatest ministers who have adorned our denomination since the days of the Reformation were educated by him'.

Among Foskett's students were three who exercised long and

fruitful ministries in churches – Benjamin Beddome at Bourton-on-the-Water (1740-1795), John Ash at Pershore (1751-1775) and Benjamin Francis at Nailsworth (1757-1799).[18] It was not that they lacked opportunity to move. Again and again London Churches looked for men trained in Bristol when their pastorates became vacant. The Goodman Fields Church pleaded with Beddome to become their minister because there were 'very few learned and popular ministers among us in London'. But Beddome and the Church at Bourton replied that there was a need for 'more learned and popular ministers' in rural Gloucestershire! At a time when hymn singing was still a matter of public controversy, all three of these men contributed many hymns to the worship of their churches.[19] Beddome composed a hymn each week to be sung after the sermon on Sunday mornings and there are three manuscript volumes of his hymns in the present College Library. Francis wrote more than 200 hymns, while John Ash, along with Caleb Evans, compiled a collection of 412 hymns. Later in the century John Rippon and John Ryland also published volumes of hymns. It may be that these men had been influenced in this by Foskett who had been baptised in the church at Little Wild Street, London, where Benjamin Keach first introduced hymn singing to Baptists. Foskett introduced the practice of hymn singing to his Church at Alcester, though there is no evidence of his having written any hymns himself.

In the literary and educational spheres Foskett's men also made notable contributions. John Ash wrote works on English grammar, a two-volume English dictionary and a treatise on education. As a result he was awarded an honorary degree of LL.D., by Edinburgh University. Thomas Llewelyn[20] became one of the most distinguished classical scholars of his day and received a LL.D., from Aberdeen University. He never accepted the office of pastor but chose to devote his energies to instructing young men for the ministry at his own expense. In 1752, he formed the London Education Society, so seeking to implement the decision taken by London Baptists in 1689, and to provide, in London, in effect what Terrill had done in Bristol. This venture was not an immediate success and it was not until half a century later that his efforts were taken up again and Stepney College was established.

Dr. Llewelyn never forgot his native Wales and through his writings and his generous personal gifts was influential in ensuring the wider circulation of the Bible in Welsh newly produced by the S.P.C.K.

Bristol's influence also spread across the Atlantic through Morgan Edwards[21] who emigrated to America and founded a Baptist College on Rhode Island in 1764. This College, unusually, was open to men of all denominations and although the Principal had to be a Baptist, the other positions on the staff could be filled by tutors other than Baptists. Financial support was given from Bristol. Caleb Evans, Hugh's son, collected £55 from 75 subscribers and in 1785 Bristol sent copies of duplicates from its Library to the American College. The College on Rhode Island became Brown University and in return conferred honorary degrees on many Bristol men.

Through its students, then, the ripples of influence of the Bristol College spread into many areas of church and academic life in England and Wales and in the New World.

CHAPTER TWO

Enlarging the Work

1758 – 1791

1. Hugh and Caleb Evans

When Bernard Foskett died in 1758, Broadmead was a large and reputable church. One hundred and twenty-nine members signed the invitation to Hugh Evans to become senior minister. With the help of the Terrill Trust, the church could afford a second minister, and after consideration of several alternatives they invited Hugh's son, Caleb.[22] It must be extremely rare in the history of our Baptist Churches for a father and son to be co-pastors of one church, yet for twenty-three years Hugh and Caleb exercised a joint ministry at Broadmead and developed the work of the College. It says something about the character of both that they worked harmoniously for so long. 'The influence of the father was apostolic, the popularity of the son was proverbial', wrote John Rippon.

Hugh Evans is described as a man with a 'strong masculine good sense, directed by fervent piety and an ardent zeal for the glory of God'. He was an outgoing personality with a genuine love for people. He was an eloquent and forthright Welsh preacher, always preaching without notes, and his gift of prayer was uncommon; nobody heard him pray twice alike. Of his influence as a tutor Rippon wrote: 'He led his disciples into the fields of science by a method in which hourly acquisitions brought new pleasure and enabled us to pursue from thought to thought with tranquillity and delight.'

Caleb was the son of Hugh by his first wife, but she died when he was fourteen, and his father married again – another lady from Broadmead, Mrs. Ann Ward. Hugh Evans always hoped that his son would serve God in the Gospel and so was anxious for him to have a liberal education. Accordingly he sent him to Mile End Academy, London. Caleb was baptised during his student days by Dr. Samuel Stennett of Little Wild Street Church. For two years he served as an assistant to three London ministers; then came the call to Broadmead when he was still only 21 years of age. Caleb added to his father's qualities his well-educated mind, his ready pen and his wide-ranging understanding of the Gospel. His work gained him recognition in that he received an honorary D.D., from both Aberdeen University and from Brown University, U.S.A.

During the first decade of the Evans' partnership an average of two new students arrived each year. Caleb sums up his father's aim. It was 'not merely to form substantial scholars but as far as in him lay he was desirous of being made an instrument in God's hand of forming them *able, evangelical, lively, zealous ministers of the Gospel*'. Hugh and Caleb were far from complacent; they saw the need for enlarging the work of the College.[23]

2. *The Foundation of the Bristol Education Society: 1770*[24]

It has long been a matter of complaint that there is a great scarcity of ministers to supply the congregation of the Baptist denomination. Many of those who have been called to the ministry among them have been unable, for want of provision for their support, to prosecute their preparatory studies which would have enabled them to exercise their ministerial gifts with more general acceptance. To supply this defect a small number of pupils have for many years past been instructed in various branches of knowledge in Bristol. But many of them owing to the scantiness of the present provision for the support of this seminary have been obliged to break off their studies very abruptly to make room for others. Notwithstanding which dis-advantage it is presumed that Baptist churches in various parts of the Kingdom have experienced the utility of the institution.

So wrote Hugh and Caleb Evans to the Baptist Churches in England and Wales in 1770. The letter was also signed by the ministers of the Pithay Church, John Tommas and James Newton. It reveals that there was in many churches a desire for an educated ministry which could not be met at that time. There were students, but not as many as were needed, and there was insufficient money to enable them to stay in College as long as they ought if they were to be equipped to serve the churches.

The appeal was addressed to Baptists throughout the land to share in the work which had been started by one man, Edward Terrill, and supported and continued by one church. Without weakening this link with Broadmead, individuals, and other churches were now invited to become involved in the whole policy of ministerial education by becoming members of the *Bristol Education Society*. During the eighteenth century many voluntary societies were founded bringing together people who shared a concern for some great cause (e.g., the abolition of slavery, overseas mission, the translation and circulation of the Scriptures). Education for the Baptist ministry now became the care and concern of a wider circle through the formation of the *Bristol Education Society*. The memorial tablet to Caleb Evans in the small lecture room in the present College pays tribute to him by describing him as *Societatis Bristoliensis Parens et Auctor* – Father and Originator of the Bristol Society. This Society remains, to this day, the official governing body of the College.

During the first year £470 was raised for capital investment and seventy annual subscriptions amounting to £100 were promised. Most of the seventy subscribers were laymen though sixteen were former students of the College. The Rt. Hon. Frederick Bull, who became Lord Mayor of London in 1774, and M.P. for the City of London, donated a hundred guineas, and thereafter subscribed three guineas annually. Most subscribers gave one or two guineas a year – a substantial sum in those days. This qualified them to become voting members of the Society. Many supporters lived in the West Country; others lived as far afield as London, Worcestershire, Hampshire and Leicestershire – an indication of the widespread interest in education for the ministry.

The aims of the Society were defined as:

1. To supply destitute congregations with a succession of able and evangelical ministers.
2. To assist young men of promising ability for the ministry in such a course of preparatory study as may enable them with the blessing of God, to exercise their ministerial talents with general acceptance and usefulness.
3. To involve churches in the selection of suitable candidates for the ministry. 'The Society are determined to receive no

students but such as are members of churches and are recommended as persons of promising ability for the ministry.'
4. To encourage evangelistic work in the churches.

The newly-formed Society was swift to implement its policy.
At its first meeting it appointed James Newton as classical
tutor.[25] A native of Chenies, Buckinghamshire, he had been
educated in London under Dr. Thomas Llewelyn. He became
assistant minister at the Pithay Church in 1757, and from 1770
until his death combined this office with that of College Tutor.
A cultured man, he taught Latin to Hannah More; also amongst
his literary friends was Joseph Cottle the poet and writer.

The first meeting of the Society accepted, and agreed to
support, two students: Thomas Dunscombe of Tiverton and
John Geard of Yeovil. They joined other students already being
supported by the Terrill Fund, the Particular Baptist Fund and
the Bristol Baptist Fund. Occasionally students were financed
by their home Church, or by their parents. Bursaries were
awarded for the purchase of books.

In 1770 there were nine students, but the number quickly
doubled. At the same time the course of study was lengthened
to four years. This growth in numbers put considerable pres-
sure on accommodation, for all students had lived in the home
of the Principal or of the Tutor. In consequence the College
purchased an additional house in North Street for the Principal
and his family, and adapted his original house to provide a
lecture room, dining room and library.

3. A Liberal Education

The last thirty years of the eighteenth century saw a great
advance in man's knowledge. The development in the study
of anatomy and medicine brought about a deeper understanding of the human body in all its complexity. Men began
to explore this planet, and, through astronomy, to look beyond
it. Exploration and travel led to the colonisation of other lands
by the Western nations and their exploitation by commercial
interests. The same spirit of enquiry and discovery entered
the Church and led to the great missionary enterprise of the
nineteenth century. In Britain the Industrial Revolution began
to transform society, bringing with it many questions and
problems.

These changes the Church could not afford to ignore; the College in Bristol was unwilling to close its eyes and ears to the intellectual challenges of the day. The patrons of the Society declared:

> The importance of a liberal education, more especially to candidates for the Christian Ministry, is so exceedingly obvious that one might almost think it impossible that any considerate, intelligent person should not be convinced of it.

So the curriculum remained a wide one, embracing not only Theology, but English Grammar and Literature, Biblical Languages, Science and Philosophy. Linguistic work was intended to enable students to examine biblical passages in the original; Theology was to improve their faith and morals; the Sciences were intended 'to enlarge and elevate their conception of the works of God'; Logic was to enable them to express their thoughts clearly; while Oratory was taught so that they could express themselves well and deliver their thoughts in 'the most striking and acceptable manner'. Needless to say, students were called upon 'to exercise their gifts in prayer and other religious exercises'. An added bonus of such a curriculum was that it would 'enable a minister to become an instructor of youth, by which his sphere of usefulness may be enlarged so helping him to make a better living for himself and his family'. Such an understanding of education for ministry can hardly be bettered today, and it is to the great credit of the Evanses that they recognised how essential it was if men were to be equipped for ministry in that changing world.

While there were a good many people in Baptist pews and pulpits who responded to this call for a well-educated ministry, there were still others who continued to regard 'human learning' as dishonouring to the Holy Spirit. To meet such misgivings a manifesto was printed and circulated each year presenting the case for a liberal education. It recognised that conversion, the call of God and the endowment by God with the necessary gifts, were fundamental and that no one could be a minister without these qualifications. But to rely on the Holy Spirit to the exclusion of intellectual effort was as misguided as to rely on education without the Spirit. 'It is tempting the Spirit of God to expect the Spirit to do in an extra-ordinary way what we are authorised to expect through the normal cultivation of our talent.'

Each year, from 1773 onwards, a sermon was preached at the Annual Meetings of the Society by a minister elected by the Society.[26] Hugh Evans preached the first, entitled *The Able Minister*, basing his message on *2 Corinthians 3, 5-6*. 'The able minister needs to possess a tolerable share of endowments . . . and he needs the improvements of human learning. No profession needs this more than the ministry, when such learning is sanctified and humbly devoted to the service of God.'

About four or five new students entered College each year after 1770. They came from differing Churches as far apart as Devonshire and Northamptonshire, Wales and Yorkshire, and London. One of the nine students already in residence in 1770 was John Rippon who, like Thomas Dunscombe, came from the ancient Baptist Church at Tiverton, a Church which had been led by a minister who had been strongly influenced by the Welsh Revival. Dr. Rippon, the recorder of the history of the College, is also remembered as the minister who, during a long and influential ministry in London, edited *The Baptist Register*, and published *A selection of hymns from the Best Authors (1787)*, which was widely used for several generations of Baptists. His fellow Devonian, Dunscombe, settled at Coate in Oxfordshire and did much to encourage and revive Baptist life in the Oxfordshire villages.

Isaac James entered College in 1771 and became the historian of the Broadmead Church and a tutor at the College. A year later he was joined by a man who had walked two hundred miles to get to College, all the way from John Fawcett's church in Hebden Bridge, Yorkshire, because he chose to save the money to buy books when he got there. He was John Sutcliff, later to become minister at Olney, Bucks., and one of the founders of the Baptist Missionary Society.

4. The Library[27]

Not all students could save money to buy books by walking two hundred miles as Sutcliff had done. Yet for the kind of education now being offered, books were absolutely essential.

What was needed was a Library and in 1772 an appeal for funds was launched to provide one. Caleb Evans travelled all over the country collecting gifts from churches and individuals. Eventually enough was raised to build a Library in the garden of the College house.

Andrew Gifford (1700-1784) who had been tutor at the College in 1727 and 1728, gave £100. Ten years after his gift to the Library Fund, Gifford wrote his will, leaving all his books, manuscripts and other collections to the College. It was a magnificent gift. During his long pastorate in London, Gifford had maintained wide cultural interests, and became a sub-librarian of the British Museum in 1757, in which capacity he gave public lectures on many subjects. His collection included fossils, rocks, plants and sea-weed. He became an expert numismatist and his valuable collection of coins was purchased by King George II. More significant from the point of view of the College was his collection of books and manuscripts, on a whole range of subjects, particularly his unique collection of Bibles. Among these was the only surviving complete copy of the first edition of William Tyndale's New Testament in English, printed at Worms on Peter Shoeffer's press in 1525.

Dr. L. G. Champion singles out Gifford's two great convictions: 'The need for an educated ministry, if the life of the Church is to be maintained; and his passionate belief in the sovereign grace of God, known in Christ, which lays on men an obligation to commend the Good News to everyone and to persuade them by all means to accept it.'

Dr. Gifford had ideas about establishing a Baptist College 'for law and physic for gentlemen of independent fortunes' at either Oxford or Cambridge. This did not materialise. It was Bristol College, with its emphases on producing able and evangelical ministers, which benefited from his munificent generosity. He did, however, express the hope that the College would apply for a charter and become a University, but 'owing to the modesty of the present tutors, the plan was not proceeded with', commented Dr. Rippon.

In the same year that Dr. Gifford died, 1784, the College received two other substantial legacies. Alderman Frederick Bull, a founder member of the Education Society, left 1,000 guineas. Dr. Thomas Llewelyn bequeathed his Classical

Library valued at 1,500-2,000 guineas. Acknowledging these three bequests, the College report adds: 'By these important acquisitions this institution is able to boast of a library equal if not superior to that of any private academy in the Kingdom.'

5. Links with Wales[28]

Throughout the last three quarters of the eighteenth century there was a succession of some ninety students from Baptist Churches in Wales who crossed the Severn to receive education at Bristol College. From 1734 onwards one student came almost every year. After 1770 sometimes four or five, even six came in a year. It was a period during which there was a dramatic increase in Baptist membership in South Wales, which grew from around 500 members in 1689 to about 1,600 in 1760, and then rapidly increased to over 9,000 by the end of the century. The pattern of life in the Principality was that Baptists over an area recognised their identity as a church under one pastor who was assisted by ministers (i.e., authorised preachers), who preached at various stations in the area. Very few of these men were supported financially by the church. Many Baptists saw no necessity for such preachers to receive training, clinging to the view that such equipment was 'dishonouring' to the Holy Spirit. But others valued education. In 1734 Miles Harry of Pen-y-garn and John Griffiths of Pontypool set up a seminary at Trosnant,[29] near Pontypool, to afford some basic education to candidates for the ministry. Joshua Thomas, historian of the Churches in Wales, estimated the total number of students as twenty-five, of whom no less than eighteen proceeded to Bristol College for further training.

After John Griffiths left for America in 1761, Trosnant languished; it had difficulty in obtaining adequately qualified tutors and financial support from the churches; it finally closed in 1770, when the Bristol Education Society was founded.

Not all the Welsh students stayed for a full course at Bristol. Some returned after a brief period, finding life difficult in a large city. These men never became pastors: they were content to remain preachers. Others spent four years in Bristol and then returned to be ordained as pastors, often in the church which sent them to College. Quite a number found opportunities in English pastorates, a fact lamented by the Welsh

churches! A few went to Ireland and to America. Several were
men of high calibre: e.g., Morgan Edwards (1752), Thomas
Llewelyn (1741), Benjamin Francis (1753), William Richards
(1775) and Morgan John Rhys (1782).

Over the years men came from about twenty-five churches
throughout South Wales but the majority came from four
churches: Pen-y-garn (Pontypool), Pentre-newydd (Radnorshire), Pen-y-fai (Bridgend) and Llangloffan (Pembrokeshire).

Undoubtedly the closest link between South Wales and
Bristol was Hugh Evans, a member of a family which had had
an influential place in the very early history of Baptists in Wales.
A succession of the Evans family ministered at Pentre-newydd
in Radnorshire. Several members of the family came to Bristol
for training. Hugh Evans was able to preach fluently in Welsh,
and regularly attended the annual meetings of the Welsh
Association. Over the years he preached eighteen times,
sometimes in English, sometimes in Welsh. Both Bernard
Foskett and Caleb Evans served as visiting preachers on several
occasions.

Thus Bristol had a significant place in education for the
ministry in Wales until the foundation of the South Wales
Baptist College by Micah Thomas,[45] in 1807.

6. Evangelical Calvinism[30]

There is no doubt that under Foskett and the Evanses the
College was intent on sending men into the ministry who were
able, whose outlook had been broadened by a liberal education;
but were they *evangelical*?

In the eighteenth century Christians tended to move towards
theological extremes. In some of the academies dogmatism in
theology was frowned upon and open-mindedness welcomed.
But freedom from the constraints of an external authority
easily led to doubt and scepticism. Many Dissenters, including
many General Baptists, became Arians or Unitarians, denying
the divinity of Christ and the doctrine of the Trinity and
calling in question the efficacy of Christ's death, and His
salvation. Preaching tended towards an arid intellectualism,
devoid of emotion, and lacking any sense of urgent mission.

The Methodist Evangelical Revival was a reaction against
this spirit. Theologically John Wesley was an Arminian,

believing that the grace of God was open to everyone who would receive it. He felt compelled to preach the gospel to everyone and preached to win converts in their thousands. In 1739 he was invited by George Whitefield to visit and to preach in Bristol. The following year he founded the first Methodist Society and built the first Methodist Chapel in Bristol not far from Broadmead. The impact on the city was great and must have been felt in the Broadmead Church and the College.

Whereas General Baptists held Arminian views similar to those of the Wesleys, Broadmead and the College belonged to the stream known as Particular Baptists whose theology was Calvinistic. Such people believed that God had chosen some for salvation while the rest of mankind would go to perdition. The Gospel must therefore be preached so that the 'elect' may hear and respond; but there was no hope for the non-elect. Logically, such a view blunts the cutting edge of evangelism, for if God has predestined only certain people for salvation, then there is nothing that men can do to alter the situation by preaching. It was regarded as presumptuous to appeal for conversions. This outlook has come to be known as hyper-Calvinism. But by no means were all Baptists so theologically hidebound that they were inhibited from Gospel preaching. There was another kind of Calvinism, evangelical Calvinism, which linked the seventeenth-century tradition with Andrew Fuller, whose book *The Gospel Worthy of all Acceptation* (1785), finally released the denomination from hyper-Calvinism and paved the way for the foundation of the Baptist Missionary Society, and for evangelism at home.

The Western Association in which the College was set had already, a hundred years earlier, in the Somerset Confession (1656) insisted that it was the duty of the Church 'to send forth such men as are fitly gifted and qualified through the Spirit of Christ to preach the Gospel to the world'. Andrew Gifford at the Pithay Church 'would offer Christ to sinners'. Bernard Foskett, in his turn, though a Calvinist, similarly retained the evangelistic outlook he had imbibed from the Little Wild Street Church in London. Of Hugh Evans it was said by his son that as he proclaimed from the Broadmead pulpit 'the awful terrors of the law and the astonishing grace of the Gospel, I was brought to the very dust before the Holy God and enabled to magnify the riches of free grace'. Caleb himself, in the statement of faith which he made at his ordination in 1767, clearly affirmed his belief in 'the universal depravity of man and in the doctrine of election' but went on to see in the doctrine of the Atonement 'an effective way opened for a happy union between God and every believing soul. I receive, therefore, this glorious, heart-cheering doctrine as well *worthy of all acceptation*'. To what extent Fuller was influenced by Caleb Evans may be open to doubt. But both men believed in an evangelical ministry.

The College set about its declared aim, part of which was to encourage evangelistic work in the churches, especially in areas where there was no means of supporting a full-time ministry. In 1773 students, helped financially by the College, undertook an itinerant mission to Cornwall preaching the Gospel. North Wales too received a similar mission in 1776 under the direction of Thomas Llewelyn, and Baptist witness was begun in areas where it had hitherto not been heard.[31]

All this vacation experience was a part of the students' preparation for the ministry and the result was that men leaving College carried this evangelical zeal with them. Benjamin Francis, during his ministry at Nailsworth, Gloucestershire, spent his weekdays on evangelistic tours, preaching in Gloucestershire, Worcestershire, Cornwall, London, Wales and even Ireland. John Ash of Pershore reflected the same spirit when he claimed that 'the one great design of the Christian ministry is to reclaim, convert and save, a guilty world'.

John Sutcliff is an even more significant example of an able minister with an evangelical outlook. He came to College from the church in Hebden Bridge, whose minister, John Fawcett, had been converted under George Whitefield. Sutcliff's background was one in which this blend of Calvinism and evangelicalism was already found. The teaching in the College was therefore congenial to him and he took full advantage of it. After his settlement in Olney he came across the writings of the American theologian, Jonathan Edwards, and he was deeply influenced by them. They stimulated him to issue a *Call to Prayer* in 1784 to the churches of Northamptonshire and, as a result of the prayer meetings which followed, the way was prepared for the founding of the Baptist Missionary

Society. When Sutcliff died, Andrew Fuller, in his funeral
address, said he had come to understand something of the
harmony 'between the duty of a minister to call on sinners to
repent and believe in Christ for salvation and the necessity of
omnipotent grace to render the call effectual'.

One more example must suffice. Samuel Pearce entered the
College in 1784 from Plymouth and on completion of his course
went to Cannon Street, Birmingham where, in his ordination
statement, he made clear his evangelical Calvinism. He
expressed his belief in the 'predestination of all events, including
the number of the saved'. But he insisted that this was different from the rigid Calvinism with its doctrine of 'absolute
election and reprobation'.

Pearce – the 'Seraphic Pearce' as he was called – exercised
a fruitful ministry in his Church, but his heart was set on
mission overseas. 'I look at Brother Carey's portrait as it hangs
in my study. I love him in the bowels of Jesus Christ and long
to join his labours. . . . One thing, however, I have resolved
upon that, the Lord helping me, if I cannot go abroad I will
do all I can to serve the Mission at home.' The Baptist Missionary Society Committee decided he should remain at home.
Disappointed, but not dismayed, he accepted the decision. He
continued his evangelical ministry in Birmingham, stimulated
preaching in the villages around, and promoted the growth of
Sunday Schools. He shared in missions to Cornwall and to
Dublin, and above all continued to 'hold the ropes' while
Carey and his colleagues 'went down the mine'.

Sutcliff and Pearce, together with Thomas Blundel and
William Staughton, were the four Bristol men among the
thirteen who had met at Kettering in 1792 to found the Baptist
Missionary Society.

To balance this picture, mention has to be made of John
Collett Ryland who was at Bristol under Bernard Foskett, but
who never moved far from strict Calvinism. He it was, it is
alleged, who tried to quieten William Carey when he sought to
stir Northamptonshire Baptists to take up his vision of a world-
wide mission. Was he critical of Foskett's too liberal theology?

7. *Social and Political Concern*[32]

No account of the influence of the Evanses would be complete

without reference to another dimension – their awareness of
the social and political implications of the Gospel. Hugh
Evans, when he addressed the Welsh Association Assembly at
Bethesda, near Newport, Monmouthshire, in 1773 spoke on
the theme of religious liberty, reminding them of how their
forefathers struggled. His plea led to a petition to Parliament
for a more equitable treatment of Dissenting ministers. The
sermon was printed and circulated in America, where several
members of the Evans family had emigrated. T. M. Bassett
attributes the growth of political radicalism in Wales to the
influence of men from Bristol College.

Within Britain the Industrial Revolution was in full swing.
In the ten years between 1769 and 1779 new inventions by
Arkwright, Hargreaves and Crompton brought rapid technological changes to the textile industry. At the same time
Watt invented the steam engine (1769) and this ushered in the
age of iron, steel and coal. 'The steam engine worked more
quickly to transform industry than man's mind worked to
absorb its products and re-organise society.' It marked the
beginning of the factory age with all its social perplexities.
Elliott-Binns called it 'a new age in the history of humanity'
and declared that 'as always, in such circumstances, man was
unaware of it'. It would be foolish to claim that Caleb Evans
was fully aware of all the implications of this, yet undoubtedly
he recognised that changes were on the way with which the
church would have to come to terms. There were destitute
children in Bristol and he gave himself to the task of teaching
them and providing them with clothes, opening schools at
Broadmead and at Downend and Mangotsfield, just outside
the city.

Political freedom and the nature of the British Constitution
were also matters engaging the minds of men like Richard
Price, who published his *On Civil Liberty* in 1776 and Tom
Paine whose *The Rights of Man* was published in 1791, the year
of Caleb Evans' death. Caleb's concern for this area of life is
demonstrated by a sermon which he preached in 1775 on
Constitutional Liberty. In this he argued strongly in favour of the
monarchy against those from America and some in this country
who were extolling the virtues of Republicanism. Constitutional
Liberty was guarded by the 'illustrious House of Hanover'.

ANDREW GIFFORD

Reproduced by permission of the British Library

TYNDALE NEW TESTAMENT 1526

Yet at the same time he re-affirmed his belief in religious liberty, the freedom to worship God according to conscience. The people of Broadmead who knew their history and the students of the College must have been reminded of the days of Edward Terrill when such freedom was still to be won. Soon after the formation of the Education Society the American colonies revolted and their Declaration of Independence was signed in 1776. One of the issues was whether taxes should be imposed on the colonists when they had no voice in the British Parliament. John Wesley argued that this was permissible since the colonies had accepted the British Charter. On the other hand, Caleb Evans published *A Letter to Mr. Wesley* under the pen-name *Americanus* in 1775:

> Taxation and representation are inseparable. This position is founded in the laws and statutes going back to the reign of Edward I. Forty shillings a year freehold gives an Englishman a voice in the legislation of the country. Why should we deprive of this our fellow-citizens in America?

In their attitude to the Slave Trade, a very controversial issue in Bristol especially, Caleb Evans and Wesley agreed. The merchants of Bristol had become very rich through it. Cargoes of tobacco and sugar came into the city docks from the West Indies and these were paid for, to all intents and purposes, by means of negroes who had been shipped to the West Indies from Africa. Courageously, Caleb Evans, along with other local clergy and ministers, opposed this trade and supported fully the Anti-Slavery Campaign.

We can be sure that even if such subjects did not appear in the curriculum, the students discussed them with their tutors and amongst themselves. Evidence that this was so is provided by some of those who were in College at this time. James Dore who had come from the Isle of Wight in 1779, settled at Maze Pond, London, and published a famous sermon *On the African Slave Trade* in 1788. Thomas Langdon, a Devonshire man, who ministered in Leeds for 42 years, helped William Wilberforce, M.P. for Hull, to awaken people in the north to the evils of the Slave Trade. Isaiah Birt, from Coleford in the Forest of Dean, when minister in Plymouth, became a political radical supporting the French Revolution in 1789. William Richards, who entered College in 1775 from Meidrim in Carmarthenshire, and exercised a life-long ministry at Lynn in Norfolk, wrote on a variety of topics including a pamphlet, *Reflections on French Atheism and on English Christianity* (1788). He argued that atheism had been an over-reaction to the civil and ecclesiastical policy of the old regime in France. Another radical sympathetic to the political changes in France was Morgan John Rhys who came from Hengoed, Glamorganshire, to College in 1782. He exercised an itinerant ministry in France before emigrating to America in 1794.

All these men were reflecting on the implications of religious liberty in the contemporary political situation.

8. Caleb Evans – Principal – 1781-1791

When Hugh Evans died in April 1781, Caleb Evans was the obvious choice as his successor. Broadmead Church was unanimous. As a pastor and leader of his people he was well respected, faithful and hardworking. John Tommas described his sermons as 'mostly on weighty and serious subjects, composed with manly dignity and becoming warmth and zeal'. Tributes to his warm personal relationships with his students abound; he maintained a close friendship with many during their ministry. 'Dr. Evans has a vigorous mind and a generous disposition', wrote one student.

Renowned as he was for his evangelical spirit and open-minded attitude to Christians of all denominations, he was nevertheless a staunch defender of the orthodox faith as he firmly believed it. He was involved in a defence of the Trinitarian faith in controversy with E. Harwood. He published sermons on *The Scripture Doctrine of the Deity of the Son and the Holy Spirit* (1766) and four discourses on *Christ Crucified: or the Scripture Doctrine of the Atonement illustrated and defended* (1778), which went into nine editions.

Caleb Evans and James Newton, the classical tutor, were joined in 1785 by a brilliant young tutor, who shared his Principal's concern for social issues and was theologically avant-garde. Robert Hall[33] became a student at Bristol in 1778 at the age of fourteen! After completing his course he went on to King's College, Aberdeen, and became a distinguished classical scholar. At the age of twenty-one he was invited back to become assistant minister at Broadmead and tutor in the College. At once the power of his eloquent preaching was felt in the city and many leading citizens, including clergymen, are said to have visited Broadmead to listen to him. His influence on the students, many of whom were as old as he, was also great. But soon there began to arise fears about him. Whereas the Evanses had combined their Calvinist Theology with an evangelical outlook, Hall found Calvinism too much of a strait-jacket for his vigorous mind. Indeed there were fears expressed, possibly shared by Caleb Evans himself, that he was tending towards Unitarianism and he was advised to be more cautious, advice which, perhaps on account of his youth, he declined to take. Others supported him whole-heartedly, and he was in danger of being spoiled by flattery. A delicate situation which arose in Broadmead was saved by his accepting an invitation in 1791 to become minister at St. Andrew's Street Church, Cambridge. But there is nothing to suggest that there was any serious breach between Principal and Tutor.

A year before Robert Hall became tutor, Joseph Kinghorn[34] entered College. Kinghorn's letters home to his father in Yorkshire reveal a good deal about life in the College. It appears that the rising bell was rung at six a.m. College prayers in the Library were at eight, and presumably there was breakfast between. There followed classical studies under James Newton who faithfully combined pastoral work at the Pithay Church with teaching Classics in the College from 1770 until his death in 1790. Kinghorn says he appreciated these lectures but thought that 'a single passage of the New Testament is worth a shipload of Classics'. Of his fellow-students he wrote home: 'There are many tempers and dispositions . . . one or two by their levity give offence to the remainder. We generally shun them!'

Half of the students were Welsh and some of them could not speak English well enough to be sent out preaching. Kinghorn, however, relates his own preaching engagements at Fishponds, Hanham, Keynsham, Malmesbury, Thornbury and Fairford. Sermon class even then held its terrors. He had to preach in the 'vestry' at Broadmead in the presence of members of the church. Chidden sympathetically by one of the deacons for speaking too quietly, he replied, 'Preaching before

students when we expect to be torn to pieces is a painful
experience' – a sentiment which has been echoed by many a
student since! A fellow-student was critical because he had
preached for too long – fifty minutes! In his final year the
College asked him to catalogue the now substantial library,
which he did, and received an honorarium of 20 guineas. He
became minister at St. Mary's, Norwich, for 45 years.

A fellow-student of Joseph Kinghorn's was Joseph Hughes,[35]
from Little Wild Street Church, London. After leaving Bristol
he proceeded, as a Ward Scholar,[36] to King's College, Aberdeen
and thence to Edinburgh. In July 1791, Broadmead, at the
request of Dr. Evans, invited him to become a temporary
assistant to him. Caleb Evans was ill at the time, and died the
following August. Suddenly Hughes, at the age of twenty-one,
found himself thrust into tremendous responsibilities, for what
was the longest interregnum in the three centuries of the
College's life. Amongst the students who entered at this period
were William Staughton[37] and John Foster, the celebrated
essayist. William Staughton exercised his ministry in America and founded the *Philadelphian Baptist Education Society*
which developed ministerial education in the mid-American
States on a similar pattern to that at Bristol. Eventually the
college became Columbian University. W. Robertson Nicoll,
in a lecture given to the College and published in the *British
Weekly* in October 1910, said of Foster: 'He ranks along with
Coleridge as, on the whole, the most powerful Christian force in
the first half of the nineteenth century.'[38]

Academic excellence, evangelical fervour, and a social conscience quickened by the Gospel – these are the characteristics
which marked the period of Hugh and Caleb Evans, an era
which came to a close with the death of Caleb in 1791 at the
early age of 54. As good a tribute as any came from James
Hinton, a fellow-student and life-long friend of Kinghorn,
who had become minister at New Road, Oxford. He wrote to
a friend:

> Our denomination is clearly indebted more to that Academy
> than to any one source of benefit besides. If I had £10,000 to
> found a public good, one fourth should certainly go thither at
> once.

CHAPTER THREE

Widening the Horizons

1792 – 1825

1. Dr. John Ryland[39]

Edward Terrill would have looked with wide-eyed approval
at the next candidate for the leadership of Bristol Academy.
At the age of five he had read the twenty-third Psalm in
Hebrew to James Hervey, a celebrated scholar. By the time he
was eleven he was reported to have read Genesis in Hebrew
five times and the entire Greek Testament, as well as showing
devotion to the ancient classics. Here was the man to continue
the tradition of the College when Caleb Evans died. At the age
of forty, John Ryland (1753-1825) was invited to become
minister of Broadmead and President of the Bristol Education
Society.

He was the son of John Collett Ryland, minister of the
College Lane Church, Northampton, where he also ran a
school which had a very high reputation. There, young John
received his formal education; evidently his father decided not
to send him to his old College at Bristol. He worked as assistant
to his father at College Lane for fifteen years, and then succeeded him in 1786. He baptised William Carey. Brown
University conferred on John Ryland the degree of M.A., when
he was twenty, and D.D., when he was thirty-nine.

An able minister indeed, he was well skilled in the original
tongues. He was evangelical, too. He was one of the group of
Northamptonshire ministers who responded to the stimulus of
Jonathan Edwards, and alike in thought, prayer and action,
he had quickened the life of the Churches in evangelistic zeal
both at home and in the formation of the Baptist Missionary
Society. His Calvinistic emphasis on the sovereign grace of
God gave him a strong sense of the purpose of God in his life
and led him to a disciplined study of the Scriptures and

theology. All this provided a powerful incentive to evangelism and a guiding light for Christian conduct.

Dr. Ryland believed in an educated ministry. 'It is highly expedient that every large body of Christians should possess some learned ministers and the greater their numbers and attainment the better', he said in an address to Stepney Academy in 1812.[40] 'An illiterate, though pious ministry must be exposed to needless contempt.' In this outlook, of course, he was wholly supported by the Bristol Education Society itself which also reiterated its belief in the need for higher educational standards to keep pace with the improving standards of both church members and ministers in other denominations. What was required was not just a narrowly theological education, excellent and important though that might be, but a wide and deep grasp of all branches of human knowledge so that well-informed and well-trained minds might be brought to the service of the Gospel.[41]

Not surprisingly, Ryland himself taught his students Hebrew, Greek and Latin, but he also taught Theology, Church History, Sacred Antiquity, Rhetoric and Logic. In these latter subjects he used what modern teachers would call the seminar method. He prescribed a book to be read by the students in the class and then discussed its contents with them. This was apparently a new method of teaching, at least for Bristol Academy, for one of his students, William Rhodes, seems to be answering an implied criticism that his teacher never produced lectures of his own, when he wrote: 'If it was any defect at all, it was compensated to a very great extent by his preaching, . . . which was of a highly, vigorous and intellectual, as well as very devotional, cast. We thus received of him his enlarged and luminous views of nearly all the great topics of Divine Truth.'[42]

In his teaching, Ryland was assisted at first by Joseph Hughes, who had carried responsibility for the College between the death of Caleb Evans and the arrival of the new Principal. He stayed with Ryland for a further three years before moving to the pastorate at Battersea. There he was closely involved in the foundation and early years of the Religious Tract Society in 1799 and then the British and Foreign Bible Society, 1804. He was the first secretary of both Societies. Throughout his life he enthusiastically recruited subscribers to the Bristol

Education Society and himself left £300 to the Society when he died in 1833. His friends set up the Hughes Fund in memory of him for the benefit of students of the College, money from which still helps students today.

When Hughes left, the Society appointed Isaac James (who had entered College in 1780) to assist Ryland. He was assisted from 1802 by Henry Page, already a graduate of Aberdeen, who had been one of Ryland's earliest students. Page became assistant minister at Broadmead and also served as Secretary of the Education Society as well as tutor until 1818 when he was succeeded by T. S. Crisp. The College also made use of part-time staff. Benjamin Donne taught Mathematics between 1805 and 1809 and was succeeded by Thomas Exley. The Mathematics teacher became responsible for a wide curriculum which included 'the scientific parts of Geography, Chemistry, Pneumatics, Electricity, Arithmetic, Algebra, Euclid's element, the use of globes and popular Geography'.[43]

The teachers had problems in view of the wide range of educational background of students entering the College. The majority of Baptists were ordinary working folk, and many lacked the advantage of a grammar school education. Yet such men were hearing the call to the ministry. Many worked very hard to improve their educational standards, but some grew disheartened at not being able to meet the academic demands of the first year. The tutors did not expect a uniformity of performance. The College adopted the expedient of sending some men for a preliminary year to receive personal tuition under a well-educated minister. Others went to the Academy[44] run by John Sutcliff at Olney, and then came on to Bristol. Similarly, in 1807, when Micah Thomas,[46] one of Ryland's students, established an Academy at Abergavenny to provide for the education of ministers in Wales, the Bristol Education Society sometimes sent a student for a preliminary year under Micah Thomas. Some of the abler students accepted by Abergavenny came on to Bristol for more advanced study. But Bristol declined to commit themselves to any regular arrangement to exchange students.

After completing their studies at Bristol, a number of students were encouraged to develop their academic potential by proceeding to a Scottish University. Aberdeen was a first favourite, but after 1806 men preferred Edinburgh or Glasgow. Altogether twenty of Ryland's men graduated in Scotland, and a similar number of Crisp's men followed the same pattern. Unlike Oxford and Cambridge, the Scottish Universities were open to Dissenters.

It seems that the demand on the students for preaching appointments was felt to be making too great inroads into the time for study. Travel was not easy in those days and even to cover a short distance took a long time. The number of appointments was, therefore, limited especially in the first year. Summer pastorates and missions in Devon and Cornwall continued.

In 1821 Andrew Leslie itinerated in North Devon, as did George Aveline in the following year, at the expense of the Western Association. This the College commended: 'They consider these operations to be well calculated to prepare students for the public duties of their future life – not to mention the good which we hope under the blessing of God will result to others from their labours.'

It has to be remembered that the French Revolution, the Napoleonic Wars and their aftermath form the backcloth for Ryland's principalship, and the international situation affected the College in various ways, not least financially. It was a period of rapid inflation.

2. *Financing the College*

About two hundred students came to College during Dr. Ryland's regime. Students were expected to be recommended by their home churches, but financially they were supported by specific funds. The numbers at Bristol varied; there were only eleven students in 1795, but twenty-seven in 1817; the average in Ryland's time was twenty. The Bristol Education Society supported about half of these; the Bristol Baptist Fund about three a year, and Broadmead Trust, one a year. The Particular Baptist Fund accepted responsibility for four students, but this provision ceased in 1812, when their support was appropriately transferred to Stepney College. From 1802 the Baptist Missionary Society sponsored its candidates, averaging about three a year. Some of these came on from Sutcliff's Academy at Olney; on his death in 1814 the existing students were transferred to Bristol. Only occasionally were students, or their parents, or their home churches able to accept financial responsibility. For each student an allowance was made to the Principal, who was responsible for his board. Because of inflation this had to be raised from 25 guineas to £40 by 1811. Personal grants were also made to students. Each year they wrote thanking the Society for their support and requesting (where appropriate) a renewal of the bursary. When a student left, the Society usually voted him four guineas, presumably to tide him over during his settlement period.

Students were expected to remain at College for the full four year course and not to leave without the express consent of the Committee. An unusual item appears in the accounts of 1808-1810, reminding us of the times;

> Insuring five students from Militia—£5.10s.0d.
> Paid Mr. Adams' fine to excuse his service in the Militia—£20.0s.0d.

The annual expenditure for which the Society accounted (which did not include the stipends of the Principal and full-time Tutors) rose during the years 1791-1825 from £400 to £1,200. The Society expressed concern that the College was not geared financially to meeting the full needs of the denomination, and comparisons were drawn with the Congregationalists – 'Why cannot Baptists do likewise? We certainly possess the means.'

Accordingly the Society resolved to enlarge its membership to include

(a) Personal subscribers who give one guinea a year;
(b) Life members who donate ten guineas at any one time;
(c) Churches which subscribe five guineas per annum which are to be entitled to a voice by messenger to the annual meeting; Churches sending students to College are expected to make an annual collection.

In a letter dated November 1811 it was pointed out that a guinea in 1770 was worth five in 1812 and that expenditure has doubled – 'Yet it cannot be supposed that the present supporters . . . possess but a moiety of the benevolence and liberality of their predecessors.'

The appeal for money was clearly linked with the purpose –

to supply able and evangelical ministers: 'Those who feel and enjoy the benefits of a gospel ministry, who experimentally know the importance of awakening sinners and bringing them home to Christ, and of strengthening, confirming and establishing believers in the faith, and who are of the Baptist Denomination, will see how reasonable it is that the Bristol Education Society should look to the Churches for their aid in continuing and perpetuating it as a blessing to the present and to future generations'.

Even so, the response from churches corporately was well below expectation. A few churches gave generously (e.g. Northampton donated £15 in 1817). During the first half century of the Society's life only eighty-four churches gave to the ordinary account, and many of these were for a year only. Very few churches gave every year. The major revenue came from individuals – personal members of the Society. Between 1770 and 1825 four hundred and thirty-five personal members of the Society had been enrolled, and in addition forty-five became life members. The total amount contributed by personal subscriptions and donations in the year 1825 amounted to over £800, whereas church collections amounted to less than £60.

It is significant that in this difficult period of our nation's history, three events of importance occurred, one affecting the College directly, the other two affecting the denomination to which the College belonged.

3. The Move to Stokes Croft[46]

Since its inception the College had been housed in the homes of the Principal and Tutor in North Street, not far from the Broadmead Church. The actual site is now close beside a large traffic roundabout and a multi-storey office block which houses the Avon County Education Authority. Early in the nineteenth century, with something like twenty students in College, accommodation was cramped, even though extensions had been built in the gardens. There is also some evidence that these conditions affected the students' health. So, in 1802, there was a proposal to extend the premises still further, but the site was too restricted. Consequently the Committee took the bold step of deciding to move to a completely new site. A property became available in Stokes Croft nearly half-a-mile further to the north from North Street, and this the College bought. The question, then, was whether the building existing on the site could be adapted satisfactorily for use as a College. It became apparent that it could not, and so, in an act of great faith and courage, the Committee decided to pull down the building and erect a purpose-built College in its place. All this was in spite of the financial problems for the College caused by inflation. An appeal for funds for the building was launched and by the time the foundation stone was laid in 1806, £5,000 had already been received. Such a sum has to be seen against the fact that the salaries of Principal and Tutor in those days were about £200 a year. For £30 a student could be maintained for a year. The capital required then, by these standards, was a very large sum indeed. The story of the building has a familiar ring about it. There were long and frustrating delays. Timber was difficult to obtain because imports were restricted by the wars, and all the time costs were escalating. After four years the contractor was dismissed and a new one engaged so that the building was finally completed in 1811.

Externally it was a plain, grey stone, oblong building. Later students asserted that the architect had modelled it on Dartmoor Prison! Inside it was homely and comfortable and many generations of students over the next hundred years were to look back with deep affection to the years they had lived in it. Ryland himself, along with the architect, was responsible for the design of it. In a letter to a friend he sketched the ground plan of the College and with obvious excitement pointed out the significance, almost the symbolism, in the actual building. The family concept of the College was retained by incorporating the Principal's house in the College. The lecture room and the library, and the museum, occupied the ground floor. Above it were the studies, and above these, separate bedrooms to accommodate thirty-three students. It was then in semi-rural surroundings on the northern edge of the city.

The eventual cost of the building was over £12,000, two-thirds of which was provided by individuals and churches in response to the appeal. The remaining debt of £4,000 was not cleared until 1820. Bristol College now had a fine building suitable for its work. The annual meeting of the Society in 1812, the year of Napoleon's retreat from Russia, reported that, 'The removal of the Academy was followed by an evident advantage to the health of the students and better observance of order and regularity!'

The museum housed the inherited treasures of the College. The collection of exhibits grew year by year. The College reports acknowledge such diverse gifts as a five-foot telescope, some Indian paintings from Serampore, a set of Indian idols, a collection of sea-weeds, a portrait of Oliver Cromwell and his signature, an original letter of George Washington, a book of Chinese prints, a pair of Queen Anne's gloves, a piece of an apple tree planted by Isaac Newton's father, among other curiosities. Of more immediate use and interest were the many books which continued to be donated to the library, some of them by the authors.

Dr. Ryland was a man of wide interests, one of which was natural history, and it was the custom of his friends and relations to save natural curiosities for him. He had remarkable eyesight, described as 'a kind of natural microscope'.[47] Volumes of his notes of his sermons survive in the College archives. Exquisitely written, in minute script, with the text in Hebrew or Greek neatly set out at the top, they were taken by him into the pulpit! They are testimony to the methodical care with which he prepared his sermons. Shortsighted he may have been physically but in spiritual terms he had a telescopic vision. His eyes were set on India and the Church Universal, and on evangelistic outreach in this country.

4. The Baptist Missionary Society[48]

Before he moved to Bristol John Ryland, minister of College Lane Church, Northampton, and his friends, Andrew Fuller of Kettering and John Sutcliff of Olney, were deeply concerned about the state of religion in the world. They and others met monthly for prayer at the instigation of Sutcliff and waited. For eight years they prayed and waited until in 1792, after William Carey had joined them, they and nine others met in Widow Wallis's parlour in Kettering and between them contributed £13 2s 6d in Fuller's snuff box, thus founding the Baptist Missionary Society. The following year Ryland had left Northampton to become Principal in Bristol. As may be imagined he brought with him the excitement of what had happened in Northamptonshire and sought to fire the enthusiasm of the churches in the West of England in the same way. He remained in very close touch with Fuller, who became Secretary of the Society, and Sutcliff. These three guided the affairs of the Society in this country. Ryland's advocacy of its cause took him away from the College a good deal as he preached in the churches, at Association assemblies, and at the ordination services of his students. He is recorded as having preached 8,691 sermons in 286 places and all this before the days of railways!

Within the College he did not hesitate to put the claims of the B.M.S. to his students, with the result that during the thirty-two years of his principalship no less than 26 became missionaries with the Society. Carey had gone to India in the year Ryland came to Bristol, 1793. Just two years later two Bristol men were on their way to Sierra Leone. Jacob Grigg came to College from Launceston in 1793. James Rodway from Hillesley, Gloucestershire, had preceded him by two years. At their valedictory service, Ryland affirmed 'the worth of a single soul delivered from death, . . . the bliss of a single converted African'. Their service in Sierra Leone lasted only one year. They were convinced of the evil of slavery and Grigg, in particular, did not disguise his opposition to it. The result was that they were expelled by the Governor for interfering in the politics of the place. This raised a serious issue of principle with which the B.M.S. Committee had to grapple. In the end, they gave instructions to their missionaries that 'they were not to enquire into civil matters, but, like St. Paul, to accept the situation and devote themselves to proclaiming the Kingdom of God'. It could not have been an easy decision for Fuller, Sutcliff and Ryland, for they stood in that tradition which could not separate so distinctly social and political matters from religious conviction. Yet, in the circumstances, it was the only way to prosecute the mission.

Dr. William Carey quickly realised that the work in India required that the Scriptures should be translated into the Indian languages. This in turn required a man with a gift for languages. Ryland had such a man in Broadmead Church, Joshua Marshman, who after studying Hebrew and Syriac under Ryland at the College sailed for India in 1795 where he spent the rest of his life – until 1837 – in the Serampore community. He and Carey translated the Scriptures into thirteen different languages, not the least significant being the version in Chinese prepared by Marshman. These were printed by William Ward. Copies of their translations and dictionaries were donated by the Serampore Missionaries to Bristol College library.

Another translator, Dr. William Yates, followed from Bristol in 1814. He was a Loughborough man who spent two years at the College before joining the others at Serampore, where he published grammars in Sanskrit and Urdu. As the Serampore College developed into a University, men of wider academic qualification were also required. William Ward on a visit to England sought out John Mack in the Bristol common room and persuaded him to go on to Edinburgh after his course was completed, at the expense of the Serampore missionaries, to study Natural Philosophy. He became Professor at Serampore in 1822 and published scientific works in Bengali.

Not all Bristol students were linguists or philosophers! A notable succession of Ryland's men played their part in the opening up of new work in Asia between 1800 and 1816. John Chamberlain of Braunston, Eustace Carey of Northampton, W. H. Pearce of Oxford, William Robinson of Olney, and Andrew Leslie of Edinburgh – all went to India. Thomas Trowt of Plymouth and Joseph Phillips from Eagle Street Church, London, went further east to Java in the Dutch East Indies. James Chater of Middleton Cheyney went to Burma, and then he and Ebenezer Daniel of Burford opened up work in Ceylon.

Dr. Ryland began to receive some disquieting information from Jamaica. Many negro slaves had responded to the Gospel as a result of preaching by an emancipated slave from the United States. As Baptist Churches began to develop on the island, there was tension between white and black Christians. As early as 1806 Ryland formed the opinion that it would be a good thing to send out a white missionary to help the lively black churches, which the white planters were seeking to suppress. Realising the need for careful legal advice in the circumstances, Ryland corresponded with William Wilberforce, M.P., who described the Jamaican situation as 'a

shocking violation of all religious liberty' and agreed that
'preachers in white skins would be likely to be treated better
and respected more than black men'. For this delicate task
John Rowe, a student from Yeovil, was selected by Ryland
and he sailed for Jamaica in 1813. After two years on the
island he was taken ill and died. His place was taken in 1816
by James Coultard of Tamworth. Thomas Burchell of Nailsworth followed in 1823. Along with William Knibb, a member
of Broadmead (though not a student of the College), Burchell
had to face the intensification of the conflict between the white
slave owners and the black slaves. The missionaries were
known to be opposed to the slave trade and to be identifying
themselves with the slaves whose chapels were being burnt
down. Burchell was imprisoned and there were fears for his
life which happily were not fulfilled. The question of speaking
or keeping silence in face of the evil of slavery had been raised
again. Christian religion and social evil could not co-exist in
spite of the B.M.S. advice which had been given in 1797 after
the expulsion of Grigg and Rodway from Sierra Leone. This
time the opposition was stronger, and Knibb and others succeeded in rousing public opinion in Britain so that an Act of
Parliament abolishing slavery in the British Empire was passed
in 1834 and the slaves in Jamaica were released. A fellow
member of Burchell's at Nailsworth, Joshua Tinson, preceded
him by one year in College and in Jamaica, and eventually
became he first president of a Baptist College at Calabar in 1844.

Robert Hall wrote of the Society: 'It is not easy to determine
whether the success of our mission is most to be ascribed to the
vigour of Fuller, the prudence of Sutcliff or the piety of Ryland'.
On Fuller's death in 1815 the B.M.S. asked Ryland to become
secretary. He agreed to do so temporarily, with the assistance
of James Hinton of Oxford. In 1817 younger hands took the
helm and the headquarters of the Society were moved to
London, with a full-time secretary, John Dyer. Ryland expressed his fears by saying that 'he trembled for the ark of the
mission when it should be transported to London and fall into
the hands of mere counting-house men'.

On the other side of the Atlantic another former Bristol
College student, William Staughton, who had been present as
a student at the Kettering meeting when the B.M.S. was

formed in 1792, was active in the cause of mission. He helped
to found the American Baptist Board of Foreign Missions,
which was formulated and run on the lines of an English
Society. As corresponding secretary he extended the welcome
of American Baptists to Adoniram Judson, a Congregational
missionary in Burma, when he became a Baptist. Throughout
his life Staughton maintained regular correspondence with
William Carey.[37]

5. The Baptist Union[49]

The third significant event during Ryland's years as Principal
was the formation of the Baptist Union in 1812. The College
as an institution was not involved, for the B.U. was essentially
a union of Churches. Bristol men, however, were involved. It
was in John Rippon's vestry in London that the Union was
formed. Dr. Ryland and John Sutcliff came from a meeting
of the B.M.S. held the previous day. They were joined by
several other Bristol men – James Hinton of Oxford, Timothy
Thomas of Devonshire Square, London and F. Augustus Cox
from Hackney. A year later Thomas Thomas was elected as
secretary, an office he held from 1813 to 1819. It was he who
drew up the resolutions which formed the original constitution
of the Baptist Union. Two of Ryland's men later served the
Union as Joint Secretaries, Edward Steane 1835-1882 and
John Howard Hinton from 1841-1866. Among their many
concerns was that of religious liberty in which cause they made
tours to the Continent.

In singling out the above events of Dr. Ryland's period
of Bristol, it should not be overlooked that the majority of his
students became good and faithful ministers of Baptist churches
in this country. One example must suffice: Thomas Roberts[50]
who entered college in 1797. After a pioneer ministry at Brix-
ham, he became the pastor at the Pithay Church in Bristol
from 1807-1841 during which time the Old King Street Church
was built. During his ministry he visited jails in the city.
In 1818 he visited the King of the Netherlands to seek liberty
for our missionaries in Java. He was secretary of the Bristol
Auxiliary of the B.M.S. and was one of the founders of the
Bristol Itinerant Society which provided preachers for the
village churches.

COLLEGE AT STOKES CROFT: 1812-1916

THOMAS S. CRISP

FREDERICK W. GOTCH

JAMES C. CULROSS

WILLIAM J. HENDERSON

In addition to his work at the College, for the B.M.S. and the churches, Dr. Ryland exercised a wide influence through his pen. His publications, thirty-four of them, are varied, including sermons and addresses. His hymns of which twenty-five were printed included 'Let us sing the King Messiah' which is included in the current Baptist Hymn Book. In 1814 he published *A candid statement on the reasons which induce Baptists to differ from their Christian Brethren.* He was by no means a narrow-minded denominationalist. He believed that the Lord's Table should be open to all believers. Good men of all denominations he cordially loved and throughout his life he maintained an extensive correspondence with eminent divines of different denominations.

Until he was 70 he enjoyed good health; in his last two years he asked to be relieved of residential duties. He continued as President and as Hebrew tutor, but died soon after rearrangements had been made.

CHAPTER FOUR

The Victorian Era

1825 – 1896

K. S. Latourette has described the hundred years from 1815 to 1914 as 'The Great Century'. It was a century which was dominated in Britain by the long reign of Queen Victoria whose way of life made a welcome change from that of the succession of monarchs who preceded her and whose personal influence was therefore great. The British Empire was a strong and powerful factor in world affairs, and this brought opportunities for travel facilitating increasing activity on the part of the Missionary Societies in evangelism, medicine and education. At home the age was characterised by the spread of industrialisation and the consequent growth of new towns which brought increased wealth to many but harsh economic difficulties for others.

Educational opportunities became progressively more widely available. The University of London (founded in 1836) deliberately rejected all credal tests, and by 1871 Oxford and Cambridge had removed all regulations which had barred Nonconformists from graduating. By the end of the period the first red-brick Universities were receiving their charters. The Education Act of 1870 promised the opportunity of schooling to every child.

It was an era of intellectual development and in the ferment of new ideas conceptions of authority came under challenge. The development of scientific and historical methods made serious demands on honest thinkers. Biblical criticism, emanating from Germany, began to threaten the foundations of belief for some people. On the other hand, it stimulated others to welcome all truth as contributing to a larger view of the Christian faith. They saw the validity of a critical approach and sought to integrate it into their own understanding of

40

Scripture. All these factors have to be taken into account when considering the history of the College in the last three quarters of the nineteenth century.

1. Broadmead and the College

When Dr. Ryland submitted his resignation from the Presidency of the Education Society a committee was set up to appoint his successor and to review policy. Before they could complete their report the following year Ryland had died. The Committee now made some far-reaching decisions. One was the separation of the College Staff from the ministry of the Broadmead Church. Until then both Principal and Tutor had been ministers of that church and had been maintained by the church aided by the Terrill Fund. Now it was decided that Principal and Tutor should be employed full-time and be maintained by the Education Society, although some income from the Terrill Fund was still available to the College.

This arrangement left both the church and the College free to make their own appointments. Broadmead invited Robert Hall[33] to return to Bristol as its pastor. He was already sixty-one years old and in poor health and clearly felt able to accept the invitation only on condition that he would have no responsibilities at the College. Before accepting, he went so far as to examine the deeds of the Terrill bequest in order to satisfy himself that the pastor of Broadmead was under no obligation to become Principal of the College. This is not to say that he took no interest in the College or its students. Indeed, each Tuesday evening in Broadmead a 'conference' was held which was usually attended by some two hundred people. Two students, or sometimes one student and the Principal, would speak on a selected passage of Scripture. Robert Hall would then conclude the conference by speaking on the same passage for the final fifteen minutes. It must have been something of an ordeal for the students concerned. On Sundays, the first hymn was usually announced by a student and during the reading of the verse, Hall would enter the pulpit.

Hall also entertained the students in his home, helping them to relax by his levity and witty conversation as well as stimulating their thinking. One of the students of the period, F. W. Trestail in his *Reminiscences*,[51] recalls his saying, 'What is

Broadmead but an ordinary Baptist Church? If it is distinguished from other churches, Sir, it is owing to its connection
with the Academy. Under God the students are the hope of
the denomination. If I have any influence, Sir, they should
have the best seats in the place and when there I would cover
them over with a cloth of gold.'

2. T. S. Crisp: Principal 1825-1868

The formal work of the College was left to others. The Committee appointed as Principal Thomas Steffe Crisp (1788-
1868).[52] For seven years he had served as assistant minister to
Ryland at Broadmead and as tutor at the College. On becoming
Principal he ceased officially to be assistant minister at Broadmead but he continued in membership there under successive
ministers; indeed the people of Broadmead never ceased to
regard him also as their minister. During subsequent periods
when the Church was without a minister he undertook pastoral
responsibility. As Dr. Gotch said: 'With gentle and sympathetic
kindness he watched over the sick, . . . tenderly he sought to
alleviate the sorrows of the distressed.'

Crisp came from a Congregational family in Suffolk. He
was educated at Wymondley Academy, Hertfordshire and
then at Glasgow University in 1808-1809. For eight years he
was minister of St. Ives Congregational Church, Huntingdon-
shire. During this time he began to feel that baptism should be
of believers and not infants. He consulted Joseph Kinghorn of
Norwich about this and was eventually baptised by him as a
believer in 1817, soon after which he came to Bristol as tutor.
Convinced Baptist as he now was he maintained close fellowship with both Anglicans and his former Congregational
colleagues, notably William Jay of Bath and Thomas Morrell,
his former tutor.

To assist Crisp, the Committee appointed William Anderson
(1784-1833)[53] as the Classical and Mathematical Tutor. A
Scotsman by birth, a native of Aberdeen, he had moved to
London as a young man and joined the Little Wild Street
Church. He entered Bristol as a student in 1805 where he
excelled in foreign languages. On leaving College he settled
in the pastorate at Dunstable, where he wrote a number of
books on topics as far apart as *The History of the Russian Empire*

(1815) and *Baptists Justified by Jeremy Taylor*. Anderson had an advanced view of education. Its primary purpose was not simply the imparting of knowledge by the teacher and the acquisition of it by the student, but rather the sharpening and disciplining of the mind. His own mind was precisely of this kind and his knowledge of both the Scriptures and the Classics was extensive. Behind Anderson's brusque Scottish exterior, students soon discovered a heart of gold, and a man whose spiritual priorities were right. Trestrail gives an account of his own sermon class. When he had sat down after preaching his sermon Anderson told him to 'burn it' – a not altogether unfamiliar experience! – but then, says Trestrail, 'in tones of deepest pathos, he implored us to sacrifice anything rather than the evangelistic truth, and that if we ever hoped for a blessing on our ministry, or to save souls, never to omit in our preaching the great doctrines of the Cross.' Unfortunately, after only eight years as tutor, he died at the early age of 49.

His place as tutor was taken temporarily by William Pechey and then, on a permanent basis by Edgar Huxtable. Though now a member of the Pithay Church in Bristol, Huxtable had previously been a scholar at St. John's College, Cambridge, presumably before his Baptist views became explicit. After eleven years of valued service at Bristol, Huxtable announced his resignation in 1845 because his views on Baptism and the nature of the Church had changed. In fact, later he became a Canon of Salisbury Cathedral. Such was his influence on the students that four of them resigned with him. As a result, the College Committee appointed three of their number to meet the rest of the students to enquire into their views on Baptism, the doctrine of Regeneration and the Person and Work of Christ and to ensure that they were in accordance with Scripture. We need to remember that for some years before this, the Oxford Movement had been raising questions of fundamental importance in the Anglican Church on the nature of Christian authority.

The next tutor was Frederick William Gotch (1808-1890)[54] who served for twenty-three years and eventually succeeded Crisp as Principal. He was a Kettering man, whose grandfather had offered William Carey ten shillings a week to relieve him of some of the need to make shoes, so that he could devote

more time to study Latin, Greek and Hebrew. Frederick's
father, John Cooper Gotch, a prominent Northamptonshire
layman, wanted him to have a full University education, so
after spending two years as a student in Bristol from 1832 to
1834, he went to Trinity College, Dublin, where he graduated
M.A., and later was awarded an LL.D. After five years as
pastor at Boxmoor, Hertfordshire, he was appointed tutor in
Philosophy and Science at the Stepney College in 1841. Four
years later he returned to his old College to teach Geography,
Latin, Greek, Logic and Rhetoric. Dr. Gotch's experience at
Stepney was particularly valuable because Bristol had deemed
it desirable to become linked with the University of London.
In 1841 a 'memorial' was submitted to the Secretary of State,
to be presented to the Queen in Council requesting the necessary authority to present candidates, and this was speedily
granted.[55] From then onwards, until the University of Bristol
received its Charter in 1909, a succession of students graduated
B.A. in London, the first being Thomas Baker. The change did
not greatly alter the syllabus, but a part-time tutor to teach
German was needed.

Crisp was Principal for forty-three years until his death in
1868 at the age of 80. This can scarcely be regarded as the
most exciting period of the College's history. Perhaps this was
partially due to the Principal himself. As a teacher Crisp was
content if students reproduced in their examination answers
the material he had given them in lectures. 'Somehow he did
not perceive that this was not the most effective mode of
teaching, and was more an exercise of memory than an incentive to our own powers of thought', said Trestrail. In fairness,
it should be said that he had personal and domestic difficulties.
His young wife had died in 1821 before he became Principal,
leaving him with three young children to bring up. Since the
College had been virtually an extension of the Principal's
family this must have been a severe drawback, although now
a housekeeper was appointed by the College to care for the
domestic needs of the students. In addition, he himself was
lame and suffered a good deal of ill-health.

The social concerns which had been evident in the time of
Caleb Evans and John Ryland seem to have had little or no
place in the outlook of the College in this period. Crisp is

known to have been a strong opponent of slavery but there is no evidence of any deep concern for the poverty of so many of the working-class people in the country in the 'Hungry Forties' as the wealthy factory owners increased their wealth and the workers became poorer. But Baptists seem to have come mainly from the middle classes and Dr. Ernest Payne points out that while at the Baptist Assemblies there was discussion of 'disestablishment', free trade, some further extension of the franchise and the political rights of the individual, they showed 'little or no interest in legislation to improve working-class conditions'.[56]

The significance of Crisp's life work may be better gauged from the influence of some of his men in the denomination and beyond it. We select one group who were students in 1841.[57] Among the students who entered in that year was Thomas Spencer Baynes, the son of Joseph Baynes (one of Ryland's students, minister at Wellington, Somerset). After completing his course at Bristol, he continued his studies at Edinburgh as a Ward Scholar. He did not become a minister; later he became Professor of Logic, Metaphysics and English Literature at St. Andrews University; he was awarded the LL.D. He was one of the editors of the *Encyclopaedia Britannica* (1884).

Charles Stanford came from Doddridge's Church at Northampton. Despite frequent ill health when a student, he went on to exercise a long ministry, at Loughborough, then at Devizes and finally for most of his life at Denmark Place, Camberwell as co-pastor with Dr. Edward Steane.

Crisp found a pupil fully responsive to his own devotion to the ancient languages (Latin, Greek, Hebrew, Syriac) in Charles Lewis from Counterslip, Bristol, a man who devoted these gifts to translation work for the Baptist Missionary Society in Ceylon and India. His wife, sister of George Gould, pioneered the work of the Zenana Mission.

The other two men of that year left without completing their courses, because they ceased to be Baptists. On the other hand in the Common Room at the time were two future Presidents of the Baptist Union; George Gould, famous for his long ministry at Norwich, and John Jenkin Brown from Pontypool, who served at Reading and then at Circus Chapel, and Wycliffe, Birmingham.

John Trafford from Bourton-on-the-Water, after completing his course at Bristol, proceeded on a Dr. Williams' scholarship to Glasgow. After a pastorate at Weymouth he went to Serampore, first as tutor and then as Principal (1858-1879). During these years, Serampore grew in stature and was one of the first Colleges to become affiliated to the new-instituted University of Calcutta. Richard Webley of Corsham went to Haiti, where a church beginning with two Christians was built up to one of one hundred and thirty strong in twenty years.

So although Crisp's long presidency was quieter than some others, the College continued to produce able and evangelical ministers. The College Committee was, however, greatly concerned at the decline in the numbers of students at this period – there were only ten in 1847, compared with the normal average of about twenty.

In building a College to accommodate thirty, the Committee had obviously been expecting an increase in numbers. That this did not happen may be attributed to at least three causes. Although between 1790 and 1832 the number of Baptist Churches had trebled, in 1846 *The Baptist Record* noted 'signs of spiritual depression of diminished vitality and power'. The College Committee, after investigating the fall in numbers, reported that 'there is reason to fear that piety is becoming less fervent and active among its numbers and if so from this cause our supply will be still further diminished, since, unless the spirit of ardent zeal animates the younger members of our Churches, few men will offer themselves for the work nor if they did would they be suitable to engage in it'. This statement is supported by the fact that in 1837 Crisp had to share his doubts about some of the students with the Committee who set up a group to meet the students. It reported that 'it appeared that there had been in certain students an habitual tone of light and frivolous conversation, and a propensity, indulged to a great extent, to introduce topics and allusions which were totally incompatible with Christian purity'. In order to safeguard the standards of the College, the Committee expelled three students and extended the probationary period of others. Greater care was subsequently taken in the selection of students and the churches and ministers were asked to recommend only such young men who could 'give evidence, by seriousness, conscientiousness and well-ordered deportment, that religion is predominant in their minds'.

A second reason for the smaller numbers was doubtless the continuing suspicion among Baptists of an educated ministry, particularly as liberal scholarship began to infiltrate from Germany. Though educational standards were rising generally there was still a feeling among some that ministry was simply a gift of the Spirit which needed no further training. Consequently a number of Churches sought ministers who had not been to College. The College, however, reaffirmed its conviction that it was desirable 'that our ministers shall appear, both in the pulpit and in society, as intelligent, well-informed, highly cultivated men, showing that between non-conformity and mental incapacity there is no such inseparable relation as is sometimes taken for granted'.

Thirdly, it could hardly be expected that the numbers of men coming to Bristol could increase when there were now several other Colleges also engaged in preparing men for the Baptist ministry.

3. Bristol and the other Baptist Colleges[58]

In the first decade of the nineteenth century Colleges had been founded in Yorkshire, South Wales and London. They arose locally as Baptists in various parts of the country came to recognise the need which Bristol had discerned. They followed the same pattern of organisation by becoming Education Societies and, almost inevitably, the majority of those first called to be Principals and Tutors had been educated in Bristol.

In Yorkshire and Lancashire the population was growing rapidly and a new sense of mission awakened the Churches. It was John Fawcett of Wainsgate, Hebden Bridge, himself not college-trained, who realised the necessity for a trained ministry and gathered young men in his own home to educate them; several of these men later came to Bristol: e.g. John Sutcliff in 1772, John Foster in 1791 and Thomas Ward in 1793. Fawcett advocated the need for ministerial education in Lancashire and Yorkshire, contributing £20 towards starting a College. He was joined in his effort by Thomas Langdon, a student in Bristol in 1778 who had now become minister of

the Stone Chapel, Leeds. In 1804 Langdon preached at the
Association meetings, arguing the need for an educated ministry. That year the Northern Education Society was formed.
Joseph Kinghorn, James Hinton, Joseph Webb and Robert
Hall, all declined invitations to become Principal but another
Bristol man, William Steadman, one of the last Caleb Evans'
men, then minister at Devonport, accepted in 1805. Just
as the Principalship of Bristol was combined with the ministry
of Broadmead so was the Principalship of Horton combined
with the ministry of Westgate, Bradford. A College was built
in 1817. There were twelve students in 1813, twenty-nine in
1826 and sixteen in 1829 and from then on it was agreed to
restrict numbers to twenty 'because of the distressed state of
the country'. After twelve years working alone he was joined
by Jonathan Edwards Ryland, son of the Principal of Bristol.
When Steadman retired in 1835 he was succeeded by another
Bristol man, James Acworth, who remained Principal until
1863 and saw the move to the new College buildings in Rawdon
in 1859.

In South Wales there was a similar growth of population.
In 1807 Micah Thomas,[45] a Monmouthshire man and, like
Acworth, a student under Dr. Ryland, became minister of the
new English Baptist Church in Frogmore Street, Abergavenny,
with the intention of developing ministerial education from
there. The College was founded in 1807, Caleb Evans' widow
subscribing £10, and John Ryland acting as collector of subscriptions in Bristol. We have already mentioned an attempt
at inter-change of students between Bristol and Abergavenny
in 1811-1813.

Micah Thomas was one of the first ministers in Wales to
come under the influence of Andrew Fuller. His liberal
Calvinism and evangelical outlook combined with his concern
for an educated ministry reflected the Bristol tradition. Unfortunately he was not appreciated by all Welsh Baptists, and
was accused of Arminianism, but J. Jenkin Brown says: 'While
he preached Christ as the only foundation of hope, he did so
warning them . . . proclaiming the fullest and truest conception of divine sovereignty and the purest views of the gracious-
ness of salvation.' He was also a man with a keen social conscience who sympathised with the Chartists. Three of his

students became the first heads of Baptist Colleges, at Pontypool, Haverfordwest and Llangollen. Micah Thomas resigned
in 1836 and the College moved to Pontypool and later in 1893
to Cardiff. George Thomas, a student in Bristol in 1820, served
as tutor from 1841 to 1870.

The links between Bristol and Stepney College in London
were less pronounced, although Dr. Llewelyn[20] had sought to
persuade London Baptists of the need half-a-century earlier.
The College at Stepney was founded in 1810 and its basis was
again an Education Society. Joseph Kinghorn was invited to be
the Principal but refused to leave Norwich, just as he had
declined to go to Horton six years earlier. In fact the first
Principal was not himself College trained, but was an able
oriental and classical scholar – William Newman (1773-1835),
who was urged to accept the post by Sutcliff, Kinghorn and
Ryland. In 1813 Solomon Young, who entered Bristol in 1805,
became Classical Tutor. Later F. W. Gotch was tutor from
1841-1845 and Benjamin Davies, who was in Bristol in 1830,
was President at Stepney from 1844-1847, returning to the
College, now situated at Regent's Park, as Classical and
Oriental Tutor 1857-1875. The third of Crisp's men to serve
Regent's Park was R. H. Roberts, Principal 1893-1896.

Before considering the suggestions made for rationalising the
work of Bristol, Rawdon and Regent's Park and Pontypool
Colleges, mention may be made of several other Baptist Colleges in the nineteenth century. The General Baptists had
established the General Baptist Education Society in 1794.
Initial work was done in London by Stephen Freeman, who
was succeeded by Dr. John Evans (of the same family as Hugh
and Caleb), tutor from 1795 to 1818. Both these men had been
students under Dr. Caleb Evans and Robert Hall. The General
Baptist College subsequently had several homes in the Midlands
becoming Midland Baptist College, Nottingham. It merged
with Rawdon in 1919.

The Baptists of Wales established two further Colleges; one
was at Haverfordwest, founded in 1839. A number of students
came on to Bristol for further study under T. S. Crisp and
F. W. Gotch. The minister at Haverfordwest, who also
served as Principal from 1855 to 1894, was a former Bristol
student, Dr. Thomas Davies. The College moved to Aberyst-

wyth in 1894; five years later it merged with Cardiff, to become
South Wales Baptist College.

In North Wales, Baptists founded a College at Llangollen
under Hugh Jones as Principal. Gethin Davies, one of Dr.
Gotch's students at Bristol, became Classical Tutor in 1872,
and Principal from 1883 to 1896. Welcoming the establishment
of University College, Bangor, for the enrichment of theological education, he persuaded the churches to move the College
to Bangor in 1892.

Three more Baptist Colleges were founded in the 19th
century, although none of them was influenced by Bristol.
C. H. Spurgeon founded the Pastors' College in London in
1856, later to be known as Spurgeon's College. In Lancashire
a College was founded at Bury in 1866 on strict communion
lines. It later moved to Manchester and ultimately merged
with Rawdon to form Northern College in 1964. The Baptist
Union of Scotland followed up the work done by James
Culross while he was minister at Stirling, and provided a
College for their future ministers at Glasgow in 1894.

The birth of so many Colleges during the nineteenth century
is evidence that Baptists in all parts of Britain had come to share
Edward Terrill's vision. But it could be argued that some
rationalisation was necessary, on both educational and financial grounds. In October, 1845, Dr. Steane, Secretary of
the Baptist Union, and Dr. Angus, Secretary of the Baptist
Missionary Society, convened a conference to consider this
matter. Dr. Gotch, deputising for Mr. Crisp, was Bristol's
representative. Steane's proposal was that the four existing
colleges, Bristol, Pontypool, Stepney and Rawdon should be
reduced to two institutions offering full theological education,
each having associated with it an institution for preliminary
instruction in literary and scientific subjects. Nothing came of
this suggestion because not one of the colleges was willing to
be reduced in status to preparatory college. Twenty-three
years later, when Gotch became Principal, he addressed the
Baptist Union Assembly on the question of education and
expressed his strong wish

> that candidates for the Christian Ministry among us came to
> our Colleges fully prepared in all the branches of a liberal
> education, and that our Colleges should have only the wide

field of theology before them to which they might devote all their efforts and in which they would find ample range and scope.

The matter was raised again in 1871 at the Baptist Union Assembly by S. G. Green, the Principal of Rawdon, and a Committee was appointed to consider it. This time the suggestion was to divide between the three English colleges the Preparatory, Literary and Theological parts of each student's course; again no college was prepared to confine its work to preparatory studies. The following year an alternative suggestion was made that a new preparatory institution should be set up in Birmingham. The Bristol Committee considered this but decided that there were already sufficient colleges and to add another would reduce numbers at the existing ones and worsen the financial position. It was felt, too, that it would lead to a loosening of entrance requirements.

The question was raised yet again in 1891 when Dr. Culross, then Principal at Bristol, was invited to give an address on 'Our Colleges' to the Autumn Assembly of the Union in Manchester. He pleaded for closer links between the colleges and the churches. He looked forward to a time when every applicant would bring not only Christian character and fitness for Christian work, but also an education sufficient to enable him to enter at once on the study of theological subjects. Proposals were put before the following Spring Assembly for an Arts College to provide basic education from which students would go on to one of the theological colleges. The Bristol Committee welcomed any larger measure of co-operation which the Union could stimulate. It approved the suggestion that local Associations should be involved in assessing the fitness of candidates for the Baptist ministry before they entered College, and asked that consideration should be given to the provision of continuing education of men after leaving college. Again, little came of all this. The colleges preferred to maintain their independence. They themselves set up an Inter-Collegiate Board but only a very small amount of co-operation ensued. In 1894 the Bristol Committee minuted its regret that so little was achieved.

4. Frederick W. Gotch – Principal 1868-1883[54]

The final years of Crisp's Principalship became increasingly

difficult for him owing to the deterioration of his health. In
1860 he moved out of the Principal's house in Stokes Croft to
a private house in Cotham. Gotch moved into College and
became resident Tutor. Though Crisp tendered his resignation
at this point the Committee, charitably but perhaps unwisely,
refused to accept it and instead engaged a number of part-time
tutors allowing Gotch to take over the teaching of Hebrew
and Theology and to become Principal in all but name. It
meant that Gotch was sixty years of age when eventually he
became Principal on Crisp's death in 1868.

A change in the financial arrangements with Broadmead
became necessary because F. W. Gotch was a member not of
Broadmead but of Old King Street, the former Pithay Church.
Later he took a leading part in the establishment of a new
church in Cotham Grove in 1872 and became a member and
deacon there. Whereas Crisp had received money from the
Terrill Fund and handed it over to the College treasurer, a
new arrangement was made for Gotch. The College Committee
and the Broadmead deacons submitted a scheme to the Charity
Commissioners who agreed that the benefaction from the
Terrill and Foskett funds should be administered by trustees
nominated by the Church and the College and the income
shared between them. This arrangement became operative in
1870 and continues to the present day.

The Tutor appointed to assist Dr. Gotch was E. W. Claypole,
but he stayed only four years to be succeeded by a layman,
Donald A. Bassett, B.A., LL.B. Further part-time help was
given by the minister of Cotham Grove, J. G. Greenough,
who taught Philosophy and Church History, from 1875-1879,
and by a barrister, Edward Thelwell, M.A., who taught
elocution on one day a week from 1879 for the next thirty-
two years!

5. *Theological Issues*

How was the College affected by the theological ferment of the
Victorian era? How was the conception of an 'evangelical
ministry' maintained in the situation created by the advance
of scientific knowledge, and biblical criticism, which called
into question the traditional beliefs of Christians? Crisp had
little sympathy with the development of modern scholarship.

Dr. Steane, in his funeral tribute, said: 'Our revered Principal held fast to the everlasting verities of the good old Gospel and contributed largely to the stability of our churches.' But Dr. Gotch, who had worked harmoniously with Crisp for over thirty years, focussed his thought a little differently. In his youth, he and his brothers had studied science at Mr. Comfield's Academy at Northampton, and he developed a more positive attitude towards the debate between science and religion. In 1851 he addressed the Bristol Association of Baptist Churches at Bath on the theme *The Inspiration of the Holy Scriptures*. His emphasis fell upon the revelation of God through 'inspired men'. Variations in the wording of Biblical accounts ruled out a purely mechanical view of *verbal* inspiration. 'It is the mind of the Spirit, not the exactness of the words that we are to look for in the Scriptures.'

Eight years later Charles Darwin published his *Origin of Species* (1859) to the consternation of many within the Church, for it seemed to contradict all that was said about the creation of the world in Genesis 1 and 2. In 1868 Dr. Gotch was President of the Baptist Union. In his address to the Autumn Assembly he boldly grasped the nettle. He entitled his address *Christ the Centre*.

> It cannot be denied either that many sincere and earnest Christians, in fear lest science of criticism should shake the foundations on which their highest hopes rest, have discouraged all such investigations and have ignored the results of them. But it is not the part of a brave or of a prudent man to shut his eyes against suspected danger. And we, non-conformists, claiming freedom of thought and action for ourselves and boasting our liberty, are the last persons who should refuse the like freedom to others.

At the time, the Bible itself was being subjected to a great deal of criticism. Already the Pentateuch was widely regarded as a composition of sources. Soon afterwards Graf and Wellhausen carried this criticism further. In the New Testament field, Westcott and Hort and Lightfoot were active in Cambridge in the 1870's, subjecting the Greek text to close scrutiny and weighing one manuscript against another as new Biblical manuscripts were being discovered. In this area of thought also Gotch was not slow to act and speak.

> Grant that there are difficulties owing to the faults in the text,
> grant that there are inconsistencies in the history – concede for
> the sake of argument all that your sceptical opponent asks, yet
> I maintain our faith remains unharmed if only we remember
> that Christ is in the centre. . . . Will our faith be vain if it is
> proved that the first book of the Bible is compiled from several
> records or if we attribute to Isaiah or Zechariah two authors
> instead of one?

Dr. Gotch continued:

> Christ is the centre of the revelation God has given us. . . . The
> Bible speaks to man in popular, not in scientific language. The
> power of Christianity resides not in the example of Christ, but
> in His work of reconciling us to God, His life and His death, as
> Mediator between God and man.

Such statements typify the reaction of Bristol to scientific
discovery and biblical criticism. It was well in the tradition of
Terrill, Evans, Ryland and has been continued down to the
present day.

It is no surprise that when it was decided that a revision of
the King James 1611 Version of the Bible was needed, Gotch
was invited to join the Old Testament panel. The committee
met for ten days every two months, from 1870 to 1884 and for
the first twelve years he was most regular in his attendance; he
regarded this as the great work of his life. The Secretary of the
Old Testament Revision Committee testified to 'his instinctive
feeling for the niceties of our language', to the value of his good
taste and natural elegance of mind, and to the soundness of
judgment always shown in his suggestion 'but above all he was
distinguished by an unruffled sweetness of temper which pre-
vailed in the most warmly contested discussions'. Humorously,
Dr. Gotch explained among his friends, the advantage he
enjoyed as a Nonconformist because 'I ranked with the Bishops,
whereas if I had been of the Establishment I must have figured
as an Archdeacon or a Rural Dean!'

6. Dr. James Culross, Principal 1883-1896

Dr. Gotch resigned in 1882 owing to ill-health. Dr. Alexander
Maclaren of Manchester and then William Medley of Rawdon
both declined invitations to succeed him. In the end it was
Dr. James Culross (1824-1899)[59] who became Bristol's next

TYNDALE WINDOW

STUDENTS AND STAFF 1900

Principal. A Scotsman from Perthshire, he graduated at St. Andrews at the age of twenty-two. Later in 1867 the same University awarded him a D.D. He became minister of Stirling Baptist Church and while there began to train men for the ministry on behalf of the Baptist Union of Scotland. In 1870 he moved to London to take pastoral care of the newly-formed Church at Highbury Hill; after eight years he returned to his native Scotland to become minister at Adelaide Place, Glasgow. He was thus well-equipped for the Principalship in Bristol with excellent academic qualifications and a rich, varied and recent pastoral experience. During his Principalship an increasing number of men offered themselves for service with the Baptist Missionary Society. To help such students he provided courses in 'World Religions' in addition to teaching New Testament, Hebrew, Biblical Theology, Church History and Christian Evidences.

When, in 1887, Dr. Culross became President of the Baptist Union, like his predecessor, Dr. Gotch, he took the opportunity to stress that an evangelical outlook is compatible with an appreciation of modern scholarship. His address at the Autumnal Assembly at Sheffield was entitled, *Dost thou believe in the Son of God?* Against the prevalent scepticism, he pleaded for serious biblical exposition: not 'spiritualising Scripture', nor 'hopping about through the Bible choosing a text now here, and now there, to the neglect of continuous exposition'.

Speaking about the 'widespread culture of science . . . which results not seldom in a materialistic turn of mind' he said:

> It is almost an impertinence to say in this Assembly that the Gospel does not frown on science and has no controversy with scientific men. On the contrary the Gospel blesses science in the name of the Lord; bids her be humble, reverent, true, and fearless; bids her learn, that she may tell again whatsoever God shows her.

The Presidential year of Dr. Culross was to prove a very distressing one, not merely because of his own ill health, but more especially because of the 'Down Grade'[60] controversy which occasioned the resignation of C. H. Spurgeon from the Union, because he considered that some members were departing from the traditional Biblical doctrines.

A good relationship had existed between Spurgeon and

Bristol College. When Spurgeon visited Bristol in 1878, Dr. Gotch invited him to the College to address the students, which he gladly did, adding to that memorable occasion by presenting to the library handsomely bound copies of all his works, and a sum of money for the purchase of his subsequent publications.

Culross himself and Spurgeon were close friends – this is revealed in the manuscript letters which passed between them, now preserved in the College archives. Soon after Culross moved to Bristol, Spurgeon wrote what is a most revealing letter in which he spoke of his loneliness in the position where he is admired by so many. 'How I wish I could be with you for an hour a day for the next twenty years. I want some over-topping companionship to keep me right.' When Culross, as President of the Union, wrote personally to Spurgeon after his resignation, graciously but firmly Spurgeon replied:

> You feel union of heart with men who publicly preach Universal Restitution. *I do not.* I mean, you feel enough fellowship to remain in the Union with them. *I do not.* The same with other errors. Still, I am in fellowship with you, Union or no Union.

Dr. Culross did not let it rest there but wrote back to Menton, Southern France, where Spurgeon was staying. Culross affirmed that for him the evangelical faith of Baptists was clearly affirmed in Believers' Baptism and in the Lord's Supper – personal faith in Christ as Saviour, the Trinity, forgiveness through Christ's blood shed for us. Why insist on the affirmation of an evangelical creed? 'My objection to a humanly drawn creed rests on my discipleship. I cannot allow any documents to come between me and Scripture.'

Spurgeon was unconvinced, and replied:

> Declare that the Baptist Union is a confederacy of evangelical churches, and that it holds truths commonly known as evangelical, and that persons who do not hold these truths are not rightly in the Union. I say, very sorrowfully, I do not believe you could pass such a resolution. Let me say that you and I are of one heart and soul. I do not think you are *wilfully* in fellowship with error, but I fear you are sheltering error beneath your wing, without being aware of it.

Dr. Culross exemplifies the characteristic attitude of Bristol to the theological issues which have troubled the denomination from time to time. The College, through its Principals and staff, have held firmly to the evangelical faith and this has been taught faithfully and consistently to students. At the same time all the intellectual skills have been employed in seeking to understand the faith and relate it to new insights of biblical, historical and philosophical studies.

7. University College, Bristol[61]

It was this openness of mind which allowed both Gotch and Culross to welcome and support a new development in Bristol. University College, Bristol, was founded in 1876 and was associated with London University. It provided both day-time and evening classes in a variety of general subjects. Very soon it had ninety-nine day pupils and two hundred and thirty-eight evening ones. Gotch had long wished that the College could be freed from teaching general subjects, and could concentrate on Theology. He was therefore quick to take advantage of this new opportunity. From 1879 onwards about a dozen students of the College were taking courses at the University College in Latin, Greek, Mathematics, Physics, Chemistry, French and German. This relieved the need for staff at the College itself, and when the Classics Tutor, Mr. Bassett, resigned in 1879 no further appointment was made. For fifteen years the Principal, first Gotch and then Culross, was the only full-time member of staff and was responsible for teaching all theological subjects, including the Biblical languages. When, in 1893, the Bristol Medical School was incorporated with University College candidates for missionary service began to undertake courses there.

Dr. Gotch was a member of the Council of University College and later his grandson, Sir Foster G. Robinson, endowed the Frederick William Gotch Scholarship available to students reading for a degree in Classics. Thus the College was most closely involved with the very beginnings of what was later to become Bristol University and it has always maintained that close association.

8. Faithful Men

Another Bristol tradition had its beginnings during this period. In 1876 for the first time a conference of former students was held at the time of the Annual Meetings of the subscribers of the Education Society in the autumn for discussion of 'all matters pertaining to the welfare' of the College. The Report for that year makes reference to many brethren 'holding positions of usefulness and enjoying the confidence and respect of the denomination'. Not until 1885 was another such conference held but from 1887 onwards it became an annual event. In 1890 there was added to this occasion a public meeting addressed by some well-known Baptist.

The missionary tradition[62] begun under Dr. Ryland continued under his successors Crisp, Gotch and Culross. Two of their former students followed Ryland and Hinton in the office of Secretary of the Baptist Missionary Society: Dr. Frederick Trestrail (1849-1869); and John Brown Myers (1879-1912) under whose guidance the staff at the Mission House grew significantly. He wrote several books and edited the centenary volume of the Society in 1892.

James Wall left College in 1859 and spent his life as an evangelist in Italy founding and fostering the Baptist Church in Rome. He baptised over six hundred people there.

Missionary enthusiasm was quickened by the opening up of new fields in China and in the Congo. When George Grenfell came to College from Heneage Street, Birmingham, in 1873, he complained that the students lacked the enthusiasm for mission that characterised his home church, and set about reviving it! He did not find his academic work so enchanting but characteristically wrote home: 'Then consider the grandeur of the work to which I repine. I can't expect to forge the weapons for so great a fight in a hurry. If I do, I must not expect them to wear.' All the same, his College course was short, for towards the end of his first year he received a letter from the Baptist Missionary Society inviting him to serve in the Cameroons and he was valedicted at Broadmead in December 1874 after only four terms. The story of his exploits in Africa, in charting the course of the Congo river in his steamship *The Peace* and laying the foundation for the chain of mission stations along it, is now well-known. For this work he received the Founders' Gold Medal of the Royal Geographical Society and the Belgian Order of Leopold (Chevalier). His compass and his charts are among the many exhibits in the missionary display at the College today.

Grenfell's work stimulated great interest in the work in Africa among students in the College. Those who felt no call to follow him supported the work firmly by prayer and enthusiasm. A Students' Missionary Association was established in 1878 as an auxiliary of the B.M.S., in which the students in Bristol accepted responsibility for fostering the work of the Society in the village churches in the Mendips served by the Bristol Itinerant Society. So churches followed with interest and prayer and financial support the careers of missionaries whom they had known as students.

George Hawker, Grenfell's college friend and his biographer, was one who 'held the ropes', serving on the Baptist Missionary Society Committee for forty years, advocating its claims by his ready pen, and building up the outstanding missionary tradition of the Church at Camden Road, London, where he was minister 1885-1926.

A number of men followed Grenfell to Africa but the difficult climate quickly took its heavy toll. H. W. Butcher went out in 1882 but died in 1884; James Shindler followed in 1886 and died the same year. William Ross went in 1883 but had to return the following year owing to ill-health. F. G. Harrison stayed for ten years 1887-1897; G. D. Brown for four, 1892-1896; G. R. Pople served 1892-1897 when he died in the Congo. Three weeks later his wife gave birth to a son, but they both died within three months. It seemed as though there were always other men to take the place of those who died. Happily, Grenfell himself survived until 1906 and Walter Stapleton, from Berkhamsted, who joined him in 1890, worked there until 1907. Robert Glennie served in Congo from 1889 for ten years; later he made an exploration of the Amazon for the B.M.S.

The Far East was also calling. In 1885 Dr. George Eaves went to Japan with the B.M.S., and worked there for ten years. As early as 1863 two students had gone to China soon after the mission there had begun. They were E. F. Kingdon and W. H. McMechan. Both, however, soon had to return home owing to ill-health. Though fewer Bristol men went to China than to Congo, those who did go made notable contributions to the work there. Samuel Couling from East London Tabernacle and James Whitewright from Philip Street, Bristol, both entered College in 1878 and on completion of their course went to China to be followed a year later by Evan Morgan. Whitewright's work was largely the training of Chinese men for ministry and as teacher-evangelists through the 'Gotch-Robinson Institute' at Ch'ing-Chou-Fu in Shantung. This was established in 1893 by the gift of Mr. and Mrs. Edward Robinson in memory of their fathers, Elisha Robinson and Dr. F. W. Gotch. Dr. Richard Glover, the minister of Tyndale Baptist Church and College Secretary, visited China in 1891 and shared in the ordination of the first of the succession of Chinese ministers to be trained at the Institute under White-wright. Later, in 1919, the Institute became part of Shantung Christian University. The Institute had a museum stocked with natural history exhibits and pictures designed to illustrate the influence of Christianity on civilisation.

Samuel Couling and his wife ran a boarding school at Ch'ing-Chou-Fu, 1884-1908, specialising in Chinese History and Literature. Evan Morgan was a missionary in Shensi province for fifty-one years (1884-1935) and was engaged in literary work with the China Literature Society. He wrote several books on the Chinese languages, and an important work on Taoism – *Tao the Great Illuminist*. He translated into Chinese not only the Bible, but also *The Jesus of History* by Dr. T. R. Glover, the celebrated son of Richard Glover. The illuminated address presented to Dr. Evan Morgan by his Chinese colleagues is among the collection now in the College's missionary exhibition.

A year after Morgan left College, Ernest W. Burt entered from Yeovil. After completing his course he proceeded to Balliol College, Oxford, to study Chinese. He served for thirty-three years in China, was Field Secretary, and wrote *After Sixty Years*, a review of the work of the Baptist Missionary Society in China.

A memorial tablet in the College reminds us that among the many missionaries and Chinese Christians who were murdered in the violent anti-European uprising known as the Boxer Rebellion in 1900 were Thomas J. Underwood and his wife, from Manvers Street, Bath. He had left College only four years previously.

All this lively interest in overseas mission coloured the life of successive generations of students. At the Missionary Prayer Meeting every week, the 'Roll of Honour' was read. Dr. Culross, concerning whom his biographer wrote, 'He had a great power of cherishing youthful souls, kindling them to the white heat of devotion', was particularly encouraging to students responding to the call for missionaries. In 1884, S. A. Swaine, F.R.G.S., who entered College from Reading in the early days of Dr. Gotch's principalship, published *Faithful Men; or Memorials of Bristol Baptist College and some of its distinguished Alumni*.[63] It was one of several books he wrote during his rather brief ministerial life – he died at the age of thirty-eight.

While this book is necessarily less comprehensive in its account of the celebrated alumni, we may here take another glimpse at a sample of seven of these 'faithful men', who shared life in the Common Room at Stokes Croft. We select the group that entered in 1879, exactly two centuries after Terrill founded the College. Evan Morgan from Wales and H. W. Butcher from Counterslip, Bristol, have already been mentioned for their service overseas. The others ministered in a succession of pastorates in England. Alfred Rendell from Weymouth went to Earls Barton; G. Hugo Heynes from Helston ministered successively at Bolton, London, Yeovil, Nottingham, Berkhamsted and Frome. H. J. Durrant came from Birmingham and after brief pastorates returned to business in his native city, but also served for many years as honorary pastor at Barnt Green. These four men may be regarded as fairly typical of the Bristol contribution to the Baptist denomination at home. Charles Brown,[64] from Birmingham, was destined to become better known than these his contemporaries. After two brief pastorates at King's Stanley and at Nailsworth, he moved to Ferme Park, London, in 1890, where under his ministry extending over thirty-five years the new Baptist cause grew to a membership of over twelve hundred. For nearly thirty years until his death in 1947 he was also honorary secretary of our College. Remarkably, fifty-six years after this group of men entered College, six met at College reunion in 1935 and addressed the Brotherhood as a veteran team.

The Victorian era witnessed a rapid expansion of churches, and in Bristol and its surrounding villages new churches

sprang to life. When Dr. Ryland came to Bristol the only
Baptist Churches in the city were at Broadmead and the
Pithay, with Downend, Hanham and Chipping Sodbury in
the adjacent country. Counterslip was founded near Temple
Meads in 1804; this church, during the Victorian period sent
no less than seventeen of its young men to Bristol College.
Keynsham and Pill were also established during Dr. Ryland's
regime. During the remainder of the century twenty new
Baptist Churches were founded in or near Bristol; several of
them grew rapidly.

Students found inspiration under the ministry of a variety
of men. They also shared in the developing life of the churches
through their preaching, joining the lay preachers on 'the
buggy round', the horse and trap which conveyed the preachers
of the Itinerant Society[65] to the villages in the Mendips and was
driven by the man allocated to the last outpost. In addition,
students served regularly at Pill, St. George, Shirehampton
and in the Cheddar Group.

Several men who left College in the days of Dr. Culross
became pioneers in Baptist causes in new housing areas, to
witness their rapid growth, e.g. Thomas Davies ministered at
East Street, Bedminster. On the other side of Bristol, Richard
Griffin, who began his ministry in the 'iron chapel' at Horfield
in 1894, saw in the new building erected soon afterwards the
congregation grow to a thousand during his thirty-two years
as their devoted pastor. William Linton rejoiced in the development at Oldfield Park, Bath. H. G. Hoare was called to
pioneer successively several new churches in the Harrow area,
near London, leaving others to rejoice in the blessings attending
on their steady growth.

From the time when Bristol men started to serve the churches
they were prominent in strengthening the Associations, and
forming new ones where they were needed. For instance,
James Hinton was one of the prime movers in starting the
Oxfordshire Association in 1802. They believed that just as
individual Christians could not maintain a full spiritual life
on their own but needed to worship and have fellowship with
others, so churches could not fulfil their true calling in isolation
and needed to have fellowship 'for mutual prayer, mutual
advice, mutual financial aid and mutual pastoral assistance'.

Thus the contribution of Bristol College in the Victorian era provided able and evangelical ministers for the twentieth century.

CHAPTER FIVE

Into the Twentieth Century

1896 – 1953

1. Dr. W. J. Henderson 1896-1922

The College moved into the 20th century under a new Principal whose background was, to say the least, unusual. William James Henderson (1843-1929)[66] was born in a working-class family in Poplar in the East End of London. He was converted to Christianity during a fair-ground revival and became himself a wandering evangelist sponsored by the Plymouth Brethren. He then became a Baptist by conviction, being baptised in Bury, Lancashire. He applied to and was accepted as a student by Rawdon College. From there he settled at Bond Street, Birmingham, in 1868 and in 1873 moved to Cow Lane, Coventry, where he exercised a remarkable ministry for twenty-one years. Within two years the church building was too small and a new building was erected in the centre of Coventry in Queen's Road with extensive ancillary premises so that a programme of adult education could be pursued. Some two thousand five hundred people attended and on Sunday mornings he had a class of one thousand working men to whom he could speak out of his own experience. At the same time he took the degree of B.A. from London University.

Early in 1894 he was appointed as co-President with Dr. Culross and continued in this capacity until Culross retired in 1896 when he became the sole Principal. The Reverend Frank Edward Robinson (1859-1947)[75] was appointed as Tutor: he had been a student at Bristol under Culross and had graduated in London University. During the following nine years he had been pastor at Bolton, Kingsbridge and Leighton Buzzard, and had also acted as external examiner for the College.

These two men then carried the College into the new

century – a century which men entered 'with enthusiasm and confidence and non-conformists in particular looked forward eagerly, for they had more liberty, prosperity and influence than ever before'.[67] The optimism was fairly soon dispelled by the Great War 1914-1918 and the subsequent years of depression. Whereas the great preachers had enjoyed popularity, now they no longer could command large congregations, and indeed congregations began to decrease. Meanwhile, the work of the Missionary Societies continued to prosper.

Henderson was only fifty years old when he was appointed. For half a century the College had been led by men who were over sixty. George Hawker describes the change:

> Our profound veneration for Dr. Gotch and Dr. Culross is not prejudiced by the admission that the climate at Bristol College has become a thought too mild. With the advent of Dr. Henderson, a fresh breeze arose, with tonic properties and something of a sting in it. For a while men shivered a little and were conscious of discomfort, but it was a healthy breeze and they knew it and buttoned up their coats and increased their pace and found life more exhilarating and more worth living.

While still at Queen's Road, Coventry, Henderson had shown considerable interest in theological education, particularly in Bristol. He had arranged for a student to spend a year with him gaining experience both in a prosperous city church and the village causes associated with it. This policy he continued when he became Principal. Each year he sent a student to Queen's Road and made similar arrangements with several other churches. In this way at least half the students gained extensive pastoral experience. In order to make this possible a fund was established in 1895, named 'The Leckie Robinson Fund' after its donor.[68]

In addition efforts were made to ensure that students had fuller opportunity for preaching in churches in and around Bristol and even further afield. As the College Report of 1895 put it, 'in order to preach men must preach, even as swimming is learned by swimming'. In these ways the College remained closely linked with local churches as had always been the intention. Students profited much from attending Baptist churches in Bristol. Like previous generations, they were for-

tunate to be able to 'sit under' a number of outstanding Free
Church preachers, men of high calibre, all different in personality and style. Dr. Henderson himself was a notable
preacher. He was President of the Baptist Union in 1907 and
his presidential address was entitled *The Guidance and Inspiration
of the Cross*. At the Autumn Assembly *Personal Value and Personal
Ministry* was his theme.

Some of Henderson's men who have survived until 1978
recorded on audio tape their impression of life in the community at Stokes Croft. Austere in material terms, it was a
warm-hearted fellowship. The personality of Henderson dominated. Gruff in manner, forthright, even to the extent of being
caustic in his comments when he considered students needed
rebuff, he educated men for the ministry by his own example
of devotion to Christ and personal self-discipline. One student
said, 'We learned a lot about the conduct of worship and
intercession from his leading of College prayers each evening.'
He took an unbounded personal interest in each man. Every
week the students held a missionary prayer meeting (usually
attended by the Principal) remembering their colleagues now
in Africa, Asia or the West Indies – for the succession of
missionary candidates continued.

This increased emphasis on practical experience did not,
however, lead to any dilution of academic standards. Dr.
Henderson required from his students at least eight hours'
work a day and, benevolent martinet that he was, he made
sure that they spent their evenings in their studies. Students
now began to read for the newly-instituted B.D. of London
University, and of the sixteen who so graduated before 1914,
several went on to take the honours degree after leaving
College. The most distinguished scholar was H. H. Rowley,[69]
who came to College from Melbourne Hall Church, Leicester,
in 1910. After graduating at Bristol, he proceeded to Mansfield
College, Oxford, and then to the ministry at Wells, before
giving seven years' service in China. He became Professor of
Semitic Languages at Bangor, and later at the University of
Manchester achieved international fame as an Old Testament
scholar and was elected a Fellow of the British Academy.

Preparatory general education was still provided by University College, Bristol, where students studied Greek, Latin,

French, English History, Language and Literature, Mathematics and Physical Science. All the theological teaching was done by Henderson and Robinson.

2. *Western College*

This situation was changed by the arrival of Western Congregational College which moved to Bristol from Plymouth in 1901. It was at once agreed that all classes should be shared. The Principal of Western College, Dr. Charles Chapman and the Tutor, T. S. Macey, provided classes in Theology, Apologetics, Philosophy and Comparative Religion, while Dr. Henderson and F. E. Robinson taught the Biblical subjects and Church History to the students of both colleges. Consideration was given to even closer co-operation by sharing a site in Cotham. This proved impracticable and the Congregationalists built a non-residential College on the corner of Cotham Road and Hampton Road. Accordingly, students of both Colleges travelled between Cotham, Stokes Croft and University College for their lectures. This co-operation between Congregationalists and Baptists in ministerial education continued harmoniously for sixty-five years, under a succession of Principals at both Colleges. It proved to be not only an efficient and economic use of teaching resources, but an enrichment to those who studied under this larger team of ministers who were competent biblical and theological scholars.

3. *University of Bristol*[1]

For some years people had been advocating that the University College, Bristol, should apply for a Charter and become the University of Bristol. In 1908 Henry Overton Wills promised £100,000 'towards the endowment of a University of Bristol and the West of England provided a Charter be granted within two years'. Other business men, including Edward Robinson, the Treasurer of the College, added their generous contributions. The Royal Charter was duly granted in 1909. Our College felt involved as its annual report recorded:

> The year will be notable in the history of Bristol, and especially in that of our College, for the completion of the Fund which was needed to secure a Royal Charter for our University; and we have to congratulate ourselves and all the West of England

that we now have the University of Bristol with a full equipment of teaching power and with authority to confer degrees. From the outset the Colleges and the new University worked closely together. The Senate of the University at once designated the Baptist College and Western College as 'Associated Colleges of the University of Bristol' for the purpose of instruction in Hebrew, Aramaic, Syriac, Hellenistic Greek, Ecclesiastical History, Patristic Texts, Comparative Religion, Philosophy of Theism, Biblical and General Ethics. The four members of the Colleges' teaching staffs were to be regarded as honorary members of the University staff. No Faculty of Divinity was established. Instead, Theology was offered within the Faculty of Arts, students taking the degree of B.A. in Theology. This was a three-year course, the first year of which was spent in University classes reading general Arts subjects and leading to the Intermediate Examination. The teaching for the second and third years, leading to the Final Examination, was provided by the Theological Colleges. Thus undergraduates in Theology took their place in the secular University. At the same time they received their specifically theological education from men, chosen by the Church for their suitability to prepare ministers, and at the same time approved for their academic qualifications by the University. The whole degree in Theology was supervised by the Committee for Theological Studies made up of a number of University Professors and Lecturers together with the Recognised Teachers from the Colleges. This arrangement continued to the great benefit of many generations of students until the establishment of a Department of Theology with full-time Professor and staff in 1964. In 1910 nine former students of the College, who had also studied at University College, were awarded honorary degrees of B.A. Two years later the University honoured both W. J. Henderson and the Reverend Richard Glover by conferring on them the honorary degree of LL.D.

Not all who came to the two Colleges were qualified to enter upon a degree course. Courses leading to matriculation were therefore provided, and many found their way to the University through these. But a good proportion were unable so to qualify. These students shared in the same theological classes in the College as the University candidates, though they could not enter for the degree examinations.

Simultaneously with this academic work, the students were prepared for their vocation by sermon class, lectures in homiletics and pastoral theology, and elocution. Even more important was the preparation afforded by life in a residential College led by ministers who shared the life of the churches and kept before their men the ideals of the Christian ministry. Academic work and vocational training proceeded simultaneously through the whole of a student's course, usually four or five years.

4. From Stokes Croft to Woodland Road

At the end of Dr. Henderson's first session as Principal, consideration was given to moving the College from Stokes Croft, no longer a place of rural quietness, as it had once been, but now subject to the 'noise of one of the most heavily worked tramways in the Kingdom'. In 1902, an acre of land was bought for £3,000 in Woodland Road, just opposite the new University buildings. In this strategic position, the present College stands, now surrounded by the constantly expanding University buildings. Throughout its three hundred years of history, the College has moved little more than a mile from its birthplace in Broadmead.

It was many years, however, before the site was occupied. A century earlier, the move to Stokes Croft had placed the College in financial straits for many years, and the Committee was anxious that this should not happen again. It was agreed, therefore, that most of the money must be found before any building commenced. Some Committee members even suggested that the Tyndale New Testament, given to the College by Andrew Gifford, should be sold to provide the necessary capital, but this aroused such opposition that the suggestion was dropped. The granting of the University Charter in 1909 provided a certain stimulus to the Fund; Edward Robinson, the College Treasurer, promised £2,500 provided most of the money was available before the building was opened.

Plans were drawn up by Messrs. Oatley and Lawrence, architects of the new University buildings. These would have provided for thirty studies and thirty separate bedrooms as well as lecture rooms, library, museum, domestic quarters and

Principal's house, but the estimated cost proved much higher than the College Committee considered justifiable. Modified plans were accepted, providing twenty-two study-bedrooms as well as the ancillary accommodation, and a contract for £18,444 was signed with the building firm Messrs. Dallow of Birmingham. The stone-laying ceremony took place in November 1913.

The outbreak of war in 1914 not only slowed down the actual work of building, but increased the cost to £29,000. It might have been wiser to have built earlier and borrowed the capital, though no one could foresee this at the time. The entire cost was met, thanks to the extreme generosity of laymen, churches and former students who gave sacrificially. The old College was sold for £5,000, and, in 1916, the College moved up to Woodland Road. But by then there were very few students left in College. Because much of the University buildings had been commandeered by the Army, the Faculty of Arts – most of whose students were then women – gladly hired our premises for classes.

On October 23rd, 1919, the building was officially opened. By then students had returned from active service, five new students had been admitted and the College was beginning to get back to normal life. The *Western Daily Press* carried a full account of the opening and a description of the buildings:

> The new College, both structurally and by reason of its beautiful situation, presents a charming contrast to the heavy plainness of the old building in Stokes Croft and the interior arrangements embody the best modern ideas. The plan is arranged with accommodation for teaching and students in the centre, the Principal's house being on the right and the library and museum wing with the main entrance on the left. The design of the building inclines to sternness, but in the entrance hall and main staircase the oakwork has been carved to mark the approach to the museum and the library.   Therein the treasures of the College are enshrined. . . . The style of the architecture is mock Elizabethan. The windows contain very interesting stained glass, supposed to date back to the 15th-16th centuries.

An outstanding feature of the building is the large stained glass window in the entrance hall which depicts eight scenes

PRESENT BUILDING IN WOODLAND ROAD

LIBRARY

from the life of William Tyndale, who was martyred in 1536. The beautiful window was presented by Mrs. Edward Robinson in memory of her father, Dr. F. W. Gotch and was designed by her nephew, Mr. Arnold Robinson. The opening ceremony was performed by Mr. Herbert Marnham, President of the Baptist Union in that year, and the procession included the Lord Mayor of Bristol, the Pro-Chancellor of the University (Mr. H. H. Wills) and the Vice-Chancellor (Sir Isambard Owen). After a tour of the College the procession moved to the Lecture Hall of the City Museum for speeches and luncheon. The toast to the University was responded to by Professor C. Lloyd Morgan, the eminent biologist whose lectures students from the Baptist College had attended since the beginning of the century. He referred to the advantages to both parties in the association of the University with its broad field of study, with the Theological Colleges, with their more specialised field of study.

> I think it may be an advantage to some students who come to the University to find, as I hope they will find, that one may be a thorough-going believer in evolution, and yet a believer in the spiritual values which a Theological College has as its central feature. If they are led to see that different points of view need not be antagonistic, I feel a valuable lesson will be learned. After all, evolution may simply be a name for one of God's ways of working in the world. There are physical values and mental values—and why should they not go together?

5. Post-War Years

The World War had not only delayed the building of the College; it temporarily disrupted the College community. When the war began there were seventeen students and three more joined them in 1915. No more were accepted until 1919. Most of these twenty became involved in war service of one form or another. Some completed their studies and moved into pastorates, one served as Chaplain to the Forces, three became Officers in the Army, while another joined the ranks, one worked on a farm and another, a conscientious objector, served with the Royal Army Medical Corps. One student, Arnold Brown (the son of Dr. Charles Brown), who had entered

College in 1914, was killed in action in October 1916. Two former students, W. H. Spinks (1894) and H. W. Wood (1909), became Chaplains and lost their lives. A memorial tablet to these three was erected in the College.

Once the war was over the men began to return to their studies, for which, their Principal said, they 'showed remarkable keenness'. They were joined in 1919 by six new students, including D. G. Wang from China.

By 1921 Dr. Henderson was ready to retire. He had been Principal for twenty-seven years and had reached the age of 78. His term of office had seen events of great significance for the College and the disturbing years of the War. He was now prepared to hand on the work to a younger man. His health was beginning to fail and his wife, who had shared fully in his work, had died. But he agreed to continue for one more year until his successor could begin. During his retirement he published a series of essays on the Ministry of Jesus entitled, *Aspects of the Great Life*. He died in 1929. Tributes to Henderson abound. 'There never lived a man less stereotyped, conventional or doctrinaire.' His own personal background and experience allied to his innate and cultivated abilities made him into a man of rare insight – 'utterly fearless in quest of truth and firmly anchored to the central realities'. 'Perhaps his greatest gift was the influence of his shrewd common sense, his hatred of humbug, his knowledge and human nature, and his insistence that we should give all our strength to the things that mattered most.'

6. *Richard Glover and Edward Robinson*[72]

Throughout its history the College has been blessed by a succession of competent and devoted men who served as secretaries or treasurers of the Society. Dr. Culross and Dr. Henderson were strengthened by two such men.

Edward Robinson succeeded his father, Elisha, as Treasurer in 1885 and held the post until his death in 1935. Elisha Smith, his great-grandfather, had been a Bristol student and spent a life-time in the pastorates at Chipping Campden and Shipston-on-Stour. Edward's father and uncle founded the firm of paper manufacturers, E. S. and A. Robinson, now part of the Dickinson-Robinson Group. Edward joined the firm as a youth and showed great concern for his employees, providing holidays with pay, pension schemes and profit-sharing. He became a member of Bristol City Council and Lord Mayor in 1908. In 1876 he married Katherine Foster, the daughter of Dr. F. W. Gotch, who shared his interests. He was generous to the Baptist Missionary Society and the Baptist Union as well as to the College to which he gave money, talents and time.

Alongside him was Dr. Richard Glover, the minister of Tyndale Baptist Church. Glover became College Secretary in 1873 and remained in office for forty-five years until his death in 1919. The resolution passed on his death spoke of the earnestness with which he threw himself into the work of the College and said that 'no pains were too great for him to take in the administration of its affairs. He was the trusted friend and helper of successive Principals and Tutors. He gave wise and patient thought to the selection of students and watched their progress with kindly solicitude and with many a word of encouragement and good cheer gave them the priceless boon of his friendship.' His daughter, Dorothy, became a member of the Committee, contributing her discerning insight to the College affairs.

7. Dr. C. D. Whittaker, Principal 1922-1924

For Henderson's successor, the College turned, unusually, to a layman. Charles D. Whittaker had been headmaster of Taunton School since 1899 and had lifted the school to a new level of importance and achievement. He had shown his ability as an administrator as well as his gifts as a Christian teacher and was well qualified educationally with degrees of M.A. and LL.D. from Cambridge and B.A. and B.Sc. from London. It was thought that, as a layman, he would bring particular gifts to the work of the College and his coming to take charge was eagerly anticipated. He began work in 1922 but in his fourth term he was taken ill and was compelled to resign in January 1924. This left F. E. Robinson to carry the burden of the College for a time until a new Principal could be found. Dr. Charles Brown travelled frequently from London to lecture on Pastoralia, while the Reverend W. W. B. Emery of Cotham Grove and the Reverend R. C. Griffin of Horfield also came in to take classes.

8. Dr. A. Dakin, Principal 1924-1953[14]

The appointment of Arthur Dakin (1884-1969) as President brought fresh vitality to the College, and enabled it to realise the potential for which Dr. Henderson had planned. Not yet forty years old, he had already had three important pastorates at Waterbarn, Lancashire, Queen's Road, Coventry and Ferme Park, London, where he was co-pastor with Dr. Charles Brown, and had a reputation as a forthright preacher – many discerned in him the voice of a prophet. Born in Shepshed, Leicestershire, in 1884 he was educated at Rawdon College. After three years there he went as a Baptist Union Scholar to Germany studying at Halle and at Heidelberg where he was awarded a D.Th., for a dissertation on *The Relation of John Wiclif and the Lollards to the Friars.* He was well-equipped for the task, both academically and pastorally. Thrust suddenly into the post from a busy pastorate, he applied himself with vigour to his calling. He came to sum up his own experience in the Psalmist's words, 'The lines have fallen to me in pleasant places: yea, I have a goodly heritage.'

The twenty-nine years of his Presidency were years of consolidation rather than of change. Relations with the University and with Western College continued their useful and amicable course, and Dr. Dakin nourished both. Dr. Robert S. Franks had been Principal of Western College since 1909, and the partnership begun with Dr. Henderson continued until he retired in 1939. Dr. Franks was a distinguished theologian. For his rich scholarship, and the influence of his high Christian character, generations of students were grateful. His published works and his lecture notes on Theology and Philosophy were masterly in their clarity. The Reverend Arnold Sims was tutor at Western College.

Dr. Dakin's province in the University curriculum was New Testament and Church History. A forceful teacher, he brought to his students the fruits of his thorough scholarship. He had a remarkable capacity to communicate the broad sweep of ideas and to penetrate to essential issues. He liked to 'tear the heart out of a book'.

His reputation for 'inspiring' first year students to matriculate in Greek became almost a legend. He would pace up and down the room pouncing on students to parse or translate. 'Get it in, get it in,' he would say. One first year student records his impressions – 'In the Chamber of Horrors, better known as the Lecture Room, there is an air of expectancy. In great disturbance of mind I sat there with my companions in distress, endeavouring to cheer myself and wishing it were all over. To a spectator it would seem as though some great and terrible event was about to take place, and indeed it was. The students were waiting – no not for their final degree examination, but for their first Greek lecture!' Perhaps that 'fresher' need not have been so apprehensive – little did he then dream that he would follow the awe-inspiring Principal to Heidelberg; that he, above all others, would be the one to succeed Dr. Dakin as Principal a quarter of a century later!

Dr. Dakin was unwilling, perhaps unable, rigidly to separate the academic and the pastoral, and his own genius for preaching often came out in his lectures so that men forgot to take notes until he sharply reminded them to do so. As one Western College student said on leaving his New Testament class, 'He makes us long for Sunday to come so that we can preach.' Though a good deal of his lecture material was dictated he did not regard his task as merely providing information. Rather he sought to teach men to think for themselves and to be Christian interpreters and preachers. Consequently in Sermon Class he demanded rigorous thought and straight-forward expression, with attention to the essentials of the evangelical faith. In Homiletics and Pastoralia he drew on his wide experience to illustrate forcibly the need to deal with people as individuals. He revived the arrangement of one student each year spending one session of his course at Queen's Road, Coventry.

Deliberately Dr. Dakin reduced rules to a minimum because he believed would-be ministers must, above all, learn self-discipline while they were in College and this he taught, like so much else, by personal example. In a sense he held himself aloof from his students, discouraging them from running to him with all their minor troubles, believing that they must learn to deal with these themselves. When there was real need, however, his wise counsel and help were freely given and men saw the true Christian pastor revealed in his friendship and concern. No one ever doubted its presence, however hidden it might have been by his abrupt manner.

In prayers, which he always conducted once a day either morning or evening, students were privileged to hear him speaking with his God and to catch something of the Doctor's robust faith. Integrated in one dynamic personality were the wisdom of the academic, the shrewd judgment of a man of the world, scintillating wit, the skill of a born teacher and, above all, the strong sense of vocation of the servant of Jesus Christ.

These qualities were appreciated by many outside the College; in the churches; in the councils of the Association and the Baptist Union; at Ministers' Conferences. On several occasions he gave a series of lectures to the general public, arranged by the extra-mural department of the University.

The numbers of students during the regimes of Henderson and Dakin remained around twenty-two, but increased to thirty in the years immediately before the second world war. In 1919 it was decided to admit women students, although it was not until 1937 that the first one arrived – Gwenyth Hubble, a member of the Mission House staff. After ordination she served with the Student Christian Movement, and then became Principal of Carey Hall College at Selly Oak for training Free Church women for overseas service. From 1961 until 1968 Miss Hubble served the World Council of Churches in its division of World Mission at New York, and later in Canada.

9. Students from Overseas

In the twentieth century there has been a marked increase in the percentage of students coming from Baptist Churches abroad, particularly from Australia and from the Baltic area of Europe. As far back as 1886 Otto Koenig came from East Prussia, later to serve as Professor at Rochester Theological Seminary, U.S.A. I. S. Prokhanoff came for the session 1895/1896. Professionally he was an engineer. For thirty years he was an outstanding leader of the All Russian Evangelical Union centred in St. Petersburg, despite frequent persecution under both the Tsarist and then the Communist regimes. He was a hymn writer, religious journalist, and took an active part in the training of preachers. Baptist leaders in Russia

today look upon Prokhanoff as one of their outstanding
pioneers.

After the first war, the Baptist World Alliance, through Dr.
J. H. Rushbrooke, stimulated work among Baptists on the
Continent and sent four students to Bristol: J. Wühner from
Estonia (1924), Rudolf Eksteins from Latvia (1925), who
became Principal of the Latvian Baptist Seminary, and then
after 1945 went to Canada to serve the Latvian Baptist mi-
grants. Similarly, Arthur Proos (1936) ministered to his exiled
compatriots, Estonian Baptists in Sweden, and now in Canada.
After the war Mikko Kolamainen came from Finland in 1946,
and is now Principal of the Baptist College there. Later three
men came from the Soviet Union for the sessions 1956-1959:
Ilya Orlov from Moscow, Matthew Mellnik from Kiev, and
G. Nebessnij also from Kiev. They are now giving leadership to
Baptists in Russia.

From Australia came a succession of men: David Davies
(1907), who then gave a life time of service to the Calabar
College, Jamaica; A. H. Bell followed five years later, and after
pastorates in South Australia became tutor at Parkyn College;
Eric Burleigh (1924), from Tasmania became the Principal of
the Baptist College at Adelaide, since named *Burleigh College*.
Edward Roberts-Thomson (1937), also a Tasmanian, after
twelve years in Australian pastorates, became Principal of the
New Zealand Baptist College (1953-1960), and then for three
years of the Baptist College of New South Wales.

From Trinidad came Eric Payne in 1935. After years of
service with the Baptist Missionary Society in India he now
supervises the teaching of immigrant children in Birmingham.
Rudolf Cross followed in 1945, but sadly was drowned soon
after returning home. Hugh Cross came from Zambia in 1950,
and is ministering in an ecumenical team at Hemel Hempstead,
Hertfordshire.

Life in the community at Bristol was enriched by the
presence of all these men, and the College has taken pride in
its contribution to the world-wide Baptist fellowship through
them.

10. Bristol and Regent's Park College

In 1927 Regent's Park College decided to move from London

to Oxford, but since the course at Oxford was a post-graduate one, part of the College community remained in London. Graduates went up to Oxford where, until Regent's own buildings were opened in 1940, they shared the life of Mansfield College. The Principal, Dr. H. Wheeler Robinson, preserved the continuity of the College by commuting between Oxford and London.

Between 1929 and 1932 four Bristol men, after graduating, decided to take advantage of the new opportunities at Oxford to pursue post-graduate work. In 1936 Dr. Dakin and Dr. Wheeler Robinson presented to the two College Councils a scheme for a close relationship; after discussion a somewhat modified arrangement was agreed. In future, all students accepted by the Council of Regent's Park who were not immediately qualified to read for the Oxford degree would be sent to Bristol, to take the B.A. there, and then proceed to Oxford. At the same time, 'Bristol men' who had graduated were afforded the opportunity to go on to Oxford, where they would have Senior Status and be able to complete a degree in the Honours School of Theology in two years. The first two Regent's men came to Bristol in 1936, and the following year two Bristol men went on to Regent's. This far-seeing arrangement has worked to the advantage of many students of both Colleges.

Fortunately Dr. Wheeler Robinson's successor, the Reverend Robert L. Child, Minister at Broadmead and a member of the Committee of Bristol College from 1934 to 1942, was able to strengthen the links between the two Colleges during the years he was Principal of Regent's Park College from 1942 to 1958. Under successive Principals between 1936 and 1978, forty-one students proceeded to Oxford after graduating in Bristol. In the same period twenty-three Regent's men came first to Bristol, thirteen of whom went on to complete their course in Oxford. For various reasons the remaining ten proceeded to pastorates direct from Bristol.

11. Tutors

In 1938 after forty-two years, F. E. Robinson[75] retired at the age of 77. Throughout he had taught Hebrew with meticulous attention to detail as well as Old Testament and, initially,

Church History. He also served the College as Financial Secretary for twenty years and as Librarian for thirty. At the time of the removal of the College from Stokes Croft to Woodland Road, he re-catalogued the whole of the library. The massive catalogue contained tens of thousands of references and cross references, all written in his impeccable hand, scarcely ever to be faulted. Students respected him as a gracious Christian gentleman, unassuming, always patient with the slow learner, even though at times they joked about his idiosyncracies, and added to the legendary tales ingeniously invented by generations of impish students.

His successor was The Reverend Gwynne Henton Davies, a Welshman, who prepared for the ministry at South Wales Baptist College, and had a long and distinguished academic career at Cardiff, Oxford, and Marburg and finally studied Rabbinics at Jews' College, London. His speciality was Hebrew and the Old Testament, graduating M.A.(Wales), B.D.(Wales), B.Litt.(Oxon). Later he was honoured by Glasgow with a D.D. For three years he exercised an influential ministry at West End, Hammersmith, before coming to Bristol in 1938. Immediately he brought a freshness of mind to the Old Testament lectures. A born teacher, well skilled in the Hebrew tongue, he imparted not only the wealth of his Biblical scholarship and insight but his infectious enthusiasm for the living Word of the Old Testament. Always imaginative, frequently provocative, he was much in demand both as a preacher and a lecturer. He was appointed Special Lecturer in Hebrew by the University. During and after the war he was in great demand at conferences for day school teachers organised by the Ministry of Education and several local education authorities. For fifteen years he was Secretary of the Society of Old Testament Studies (1949-1963), an office which gave him great pleasure; in 1966 he was its President.

He was a founder member of the Baptist Church at Westbury-on-Trym, Bristol, established by Tyndale Baptist Church immediately after the war; he gave enthusiastic leadership to this church in a new housing area.

12. Wartime and post-war recovery

When war broke out in 1939 the Government decided that

ministers in training should be regarded as a 'reserved occupation'. However, some felt it right to join the Forces, and
numbers decreased. Eight men entered in 1939, seven others in
1940-1942, but by the last year of the war only four students
remained, one of whom remained to link up with the post-
war generation. Dr. H. F. Lovell Cocks succeeded Dr. Franks
as Principal of Western College in 1940, and between the two
Colleges there were just sufficient men to warrant the contin-
uation of classes. Despite the 'blitz' (during which the College
narrowly missed destruction) and Civil Defence duties, the students acquitted themselves well academically. During vacations
they undertook pastorates and a team worked in the stricken
area of East London served by the West Ham Central Mission.

As the war drew to its close in 1945, Dr Dakin became
President of the Baptist Union and characteristically spoke to
the hour in his Presidential Address – *What has Christianity to
say to the aspirations of our time?* His presidential visits brought encouragement to churches and ministers throughout the country.

Experience in the war had awakened a new generation to the
need for the Gospel. Kindled by this conviction, more than a
hundred applied for entry to Bristol College. A special committee was set up to interview applicants as and when they
came home on leave. Twenty-seven men and one woman were
accepted, and when they were released from National Service
they arrived at College, and were joined by those who had
interrupted their courses to serve in the Forces. The life and
atmosphere of the College community was somewhat different
from pre-war days. Many men were married and lived in
flats away from College. Generous Government educational
grants relieved these ex-servicemen and their families of
financial anxiety. The Principal and Tutor eagerly responded
to these mature students; Dr. Dakin spoke of these years as the
most exhilarating of his career. Despite the difficulties of such
a change in their way of life, these students coped very success-
fully with the academic demands. Eight of them proceeded to
Oxford for post-graduate work. The churches warmly welcomed these men to their pulpits and as student pastors. Many
shared in 'Commando' or 'Christian Challenge' campaigns.

The Methodists decided to move their College from Didsbury, Manchester, to Bristol after the war. There had also been

two Anglican Colleges in Bristol for some years; the Bible
Churchmen's Missionary and Theological College (later
Tyndale Hall) and Clifton Theological College. These five
Theological Colleges now shared in providing the theological
classes for the degree in Theology in the Faculty of Arts of the
University, work co-ordinated by the University's Committee
for Theological Studies. But no joint classes were held except
those which Western College and we continued to share.
Before the war ended, the University had decided to include
'Religious Studies' as a subject in the Arts degree, to provide
for prospective teachers. Both Dakin and Henton Davies were
appointed Recognised Teachers in Religious Knowledge.

Training in Leadership[77] was the title given to the programme
of adult education begun in 1943. Lectures extending over two
hours on Thursday evenings for two years were given by the
Principal and Tutor. Over the ten years that the course was
run, lay people from about twenty local churches attended, and
fifteen of them passed the sessional examinations provided and
were awarded certificates. The subjects were: the Old and the
New Testament; the Christian Faith; Church History; Church
Life and Management. One participant wrote: 'It was a very
worthwhile course, and we were aware of the privilege extended
to us. Several of us later became ministers or married ministers.'

Dr. Dakin faithfully maintained the College tradition of
providing able and evangelical ministers. He had enjoyed the
benefits of German scholarship and fully appreciated the
positive value of the modern critical approach to Biblical and
theological studies. In the era of Barth and Brunner he steered
a careful course between the extremes of a narrow fundamental-
ism and a shallow liberalism, emphasising constantly the sovereign grace of God; not only by his lectures and his preaching
but also by his pen, he communicated his convictions.

The Duckworth Press invited Dr. Dakin to contribute a book
on *Calvinism* published in 1940. As he prepared the work, again
and again he brought into his lectures some insight, some bold
affirmation of the Genevan reformer. Calvin's basic themes and
puritanical emphases were congenial to Dakin, viz; the
sovereignty of God and His eternal purpose, the reality of
man's predicament as a sinner. As a church historian, Dr.
Dakin perceived the world-wide impact of the Reformer, on

theology, church life, economics and politics, all cohering in his stress on a disciplined life of the Christian.

'Evangelical Ethics' was the title of Dakin's stimulating contribution to a volume of essays presented to Dr. Wheeler Robinson in 1942. Also stimulating, provoking lively controversy in the denomination, was his *The Baptist View of the Church and Ministry* (1944).

Henton Davies was appointed to a newly created Chair at Durham University, after having taught for thirteen years at Bristol. Seven years later he became Principal of Regent's Park College and the links were renewed. Dr. L. G. Champion was called from his pastorate at Rugby in 1951 to share the last two years of Dakin's regime.

Earlier in 1951 tragedy had come to Dr. Dakin's home. Margaret, his daughter, who served the College as Housekeeper, contracted poliomyelitis and died. With customary faith and courage Dakin bore this heavy blow, and then early in his retirement cared for Mrs. Dakin through a long period of illness until she, too, died.

By the time Dr. Dakin retired, he had completed twenty-nine years as President of the College. More than one-hundred-and-sixty Baptist Ministers and Missionaries were trained under him. Two of them in succession have followed him as president, and two others as tutors at Bristol. His portrait now in the lecture room was painted by Mr. John Whitlock. As President Emeritus he continued, without undue intrusion, to contribute to the College Council. On his eightieth birthday in 1964, he was presented with a *Festschrift* volume of essays written by twelve of his former students. The theme *The Communication of the Christian Faith*[18] was chosen to reflect one of Dr. Dakin's deepest concerns.

He died on 18th September, 1969, at the age of eighty-four. The College Minute sums up:

> His was a life of steadfast devotion to the Christian Gospel. His understanding of God's purposes was large and vigorous so that his concern was always about the significant aspects of human existence. He enlarged and strengthened the faith of many. In the life of the denominations he offered a sane and balanced leadership. He brought enrichment to all his students and to those who shared with him in the affairs of the College.

CHAPTER SIX

Response to Change

1953 – 1979

The last quarter of a century of the witness of Bristol Baptist College has been set in a period of almost dramatic social change. This has confronted the Christian Church with challenges to its spiritual outlook and to its institutional life.

Technological advances have brought material affluence to the industrial nations, promising full employment, growth in personal incomes, and the provision of social security. A substantial proportion of Britain's national income has been devoted to providing education for all who show promise of benefiting by it. Educational awards by public authorities have enabled a very much larger proportion of young people to benefit from higher education and this has greatly widened their choice of careers.

By contrast, the nations of the 'third world', to which the Western peoples have been sending Christian missionaries for over a century, have been threatened by dire poverty, as they have struggled to maturity in political and economic affairs. As the indigenous Churches have rightly assumed responsibilities for their own affairs the role of the missionary has been re-cast. With the development of the ecumenical movement, and greater facilities for travel, Christians have become aware of the World Church as the great new fact of our time, and of tensions and challenges which accompany it. The aspirations in more recent years have been tempered by escalating inflation and by the realisation that permanent full employment may not lie within the grasp of even the best planned economies. Voluntary societies, including Churches and Theological Colleges, have been vulnerable financially despite the response of Christian Stewardship.

More significant has been the effect on the moral and

spiritual outlook of people. To speak of this as a 'secular age' may imply that people have been turning their backs on God, and measuring the quality of life entirely in this-worldly terms. This has been so. Many have disputed traditional values and sought intellectually to justify their thinking. The permissive society, at first attractive to many, has come to reveal the symptoms of a sick society; marital breakdowns, violence, racial tension, the exploitation of economic power. While many have clung to a material outlook on life, others have 'dropped out' of society to a greater or lesser extent. Some have turned, not to the Christian Church, which they have identi-fied with the establishment, but to Eastern religions, and forms of meditation. Casualness in personal appearance and be-haviour have become common.

In Britain the Churches themselves have declined numeri-cally and many have failed to enlist the younger generation. This has inevitably meant a decline in numbers offering for the Christian ministry.

But this is not the whole of the picture. The word 'secular' has a more positive application. To believe in God, the God who, in Jesus Christ, became man and dwelt among us, is to recognise His claim upon us not only for the life to come; it means responding to the needs of His world. Spirituality should inspire intelligent involvement in the life of society. The Christian faith helps to make life truly human. Earlier chapters of this book illustrate that this has never been a neglected emphasis, but it has become more predominant in this genera-tion. Despite the welcome provision of a welfare state there are tensions in life, needs of the human soul, which cannot be met by bread alone. Man's existence has a spiritual dimension.

Thoughtful reflection on all this has led some to turn aside from the traditional concept of the ordained ministry, to professions such as the social services and teaching, believing they offer more realistic opportunities for Christian service. Others, particularly those within the evangelical tradition, perceiving the moral and spiritual needs of their fellows, have felt constrained of God to commit their lives to the full-time ministry, seen perhaps with a greater emphasis on its pastoral aspect.

Against this background it is perhaps surprising to be able

to record that the number of students and staff at Bristol
Baptist College has doubled in this period. The material
resources for this expansion have been supplied and the College
buildings have been enlarged. All of the students are pursuing
courses in Theology, but in response to the needs of this
secular age the College has welcomed a few who may see their
Christian vocation in teaching or in social work. Even so,
the number of those leaving College each year, to become
pastors of our churches, has increased considerably.

1. Dr. L. G. Champion Principal 1953-1972[79]

Dr. Leonard G. Champion, who succeeded Dr. Dakin as
President, had been a student under him from 1926 to 1931. He
had been brought up in the flourishing Horfield Church,
Bristol, under R. C. Griffin. After graduating B.A.(Bristol) and
B.D.(London), he proceeded on a Baptist Union Scholarship
to Heidelberg University, Germany. He was awarded his
D.Th. for a thesis on *Doxologies in the New Testament*. For seventeen years he served as a Baptist minister, at Minehead (1934-
1938) and then at Rugby until he was called to become tutor
at the College in 1951. On Dr. Dakin's retirement in 1953, he
was the obvious choice as his successor, a fact in which Dakin
rejoiced, believing that he would 'lead the College with dignity
and power'. College life had by then settled down again
after the war into the pattern that had been familiar for many
generations. Gradually and unobtrusively, the pattern began
to change, for while Dr. Champion was no iconoclast and may
have been thought by some to be conservative (not theolo-
cally but temperamentally), he perceived the changes that were
taking place and responded courageously. At the same time
he firmly maintained the enduring purpose of the College to
prepare able and evangelical ministers.

2. Tutors and Teaching

He was joined in this task by the Reverend Norman Moon,
another of Dakin's students, who had entered Bristol in 1935
from the Harlesden, London, Church. He had graduated in
Bristol and taken a London B.D., but was prevented by the
outbreak of war from pursuing a post-graduate course at
Zurich. Consequently he had settled at Berkhamsted in 1939

where he continued his academic work and was awarded an M.Th. of London University. His second pastorate had been at Small Heath, Birmingham, from 1944 to 1953.

Dr. Champion lectured on the New Testament and Greek, as well as Pastoral Theology. Mr. Moon became responsible for Church History and part of the Old Testament syllabus as well as the Religious Knowledge for the G.C.E. Western College, under Dr. Lovell Cocks and W. J. Downes, continued to teach Theology, Philosophy of Religion, Comparative Religion, some Old Testament and Hebrew.

For many years those students unable to matriculate had shared classes with our University students, and were simply examined by the College. It was decided now that such students should be entered for the External Diploma in Theology of London University and the first successes were recorded in 1957. This involved an extension in the teaching requirements particularly in Philosophy and Ethics, since Bristol University classes and London Diploma syllabus did not always coincide. Within six years there had been a total increase in student numbers from twenty-two to thirty-four; it was evident that some additional help was needed. The financial situation made it clear that this would have to be part-time. It so happened that in 1959 the pastorate at Cotham Grove, the church nearest the College, became vacant but this church was unable to afford a full stipend. The College and the church conferred and agreed to seek a minister suitably qualified to combine pastoral responsibility for Cotham Grove with teaching on a part-time basis at the College. Such a man was found in Harry Mowvley, another of Dr. Dakin's students. A Yorkshireman by birth, from Dewsbury, he had been accepted by Regent's Park College, but came first to Bristol in May, 1946 and graduated B.A., in 1949. Along with other Bristol men he had gone on to Oxford and taken an Honours degree in Theology, with Hebrew as a special subject. He had been for five years minister at Goodmayes, Ilford, and for three and a half years at Adnitt Road, Northampton. In January, 1960, he took up the appointment at Cotham Grove and the College. Three and a half years later, as the work at the College further expanded, he was appointed full-time tutor.

CHARLES D. WHITTAKER

ARTHUR DAKIN

LEONARD G. CHAMPION

W. MORRIS WEST

3. Material Resources

As the number of students increased further to thirty-seven, the buildings were becoming cramped. It was decided to provide more space by incorporating the Principal's commodious house into the College, adapting it to provide residential accommodation for a dozen more students upstairs, and several general rooms on the ground floor. These plans included the conversion of the Museum into a College Chapel, on occasions also to be used for larger assemblies. The College treasures were re-housed and well displayed in the Gifford Room. The Principal and his family were accommodated in a compact modern house built in the grounds, adjacent to the College. The enlarged building was formally opened in November, 1961, and cost £20,500. This was met by selling three books printed by Caxton in the 15th century which the College had inherited from Andrew Gifford. The most valuable Caxton was sold to the British Museum, thereby completing their collection on display to a much larger public.

The College had also inherited from Gifford and Llewelyn books on such wide ranging topics as Astronomy, Anglo-Saxon, the Ancient Classics, Gaelic, Law, Medicine, etc., etc., books more suitable for libraries where they could be readily accessible to research students. Accordingly, about three thousand non-theological books were sold, mostly to University, Medical, and Legal Libraries, and the proceeds were invested as the Gifford-Llewelyn Fund to provide the resources to expand teaching facilities for the future.

A few years previously, in 1955, Miss Katherine Gotch Robinson had endowed two funds; the Edward Robinson Travelling Fund, in memory of her father, to be used to assist staff and students to travel abroad for conference and study, and the Frederick William Gotch Library Fund, to enable the College Library to keep up to date by the regular addition of current publications. Gifts of older books and of manuscripts have continued to enrich our heritage. A notable addition to the historical and liturgical section was the 'K. L. Parry Collection' of about two hundred hymn books and books of hymnody collected by the Reverend Kenneth Parry, formerly minister of Highbury Congregational Church, and entrusted to us when Western College closed. The library was com-

pletely re-organised and re-equipped in 1962/1963 to make
it more serviceable for contemporary needs. Hundreds of
volumes were rebound.

In the Gifford Room the beautiful medieval manuscripts
and the comprehensive range of 16th and 17th century translations of the English Bible are on permanent display. The
present collection of Bibles still remains an outstanding one.[80]
Unique is the 1526 edition of William Tyndale's New Testament. In 1976 a coloured photographic reproduction was
skilfully produced by the David Paradine Publications Limited
and one of the de luxe editions was presented by the College
to Her Majesty the Queen on the occasion of her Silver Jubilee;
this was placed in the library of Windsor Castle.

The financial needs of an expanding College during years of
continued inflation were coped with through the prudence of
the College officers. Mr. H. W. Eyles, the College Honorary
Treasurer, supported by a very competent finance committee,
cared diligently for the finances of the College. The College is
supported financially through four major channels: investments, derived from the resources inherited from the past;
grants from several trust funds, such as the Bristol Baptist
Fund, and the Terrill Foskett Trust; subscriptions from
individuals and churches, as members of the Bristol Education
Society; and the contributions made by or on behalf of students.
About half our income is derived from the students, most of it
by grants from their Local Education Authorities.

Mr. Eyles, Treasurer for twenty-one years, was succeeded
in 1975 by Mr. R. A. Montacute. In the same year the Reverend C. Sidney Hall, B.A., succeeded as Secretary. Much of
the administration depends on the College Secretary under the
direction of the College Committee, which guides the policy of
the College and selects the students. Mr. Hall also continues to
serve the Bristol College Brotherhood which links former
students in a bond of fellowship which finds corporate expression in half-yearly reunions during the College meetings in
October and the Baptist Union annual assembly. The 'Gesture
Fund', started and administered by the Reverend A. J.
Westlake in 1935 (and since 1953 by Sidney Hall), has ministered to many former Bristol students in times of illness or
bereavement.

4. The University of Bristol and the Theological Colleges

New developments took place in the University which culminated in the establishment of a Department of Theology within the Faculty of Arts. During the post-war years in addition to ministerial candidates a few people came up to the University to read Theology without intention of proceeding to ordination. Such students had been obliged to choose at which of the five Theological Colleges they would read for their second and third years. In full consultation with the Theological Colleges, a Department of Theology was established in 1964 and the Professor appointed. He was the Reverend Kenneth Grayston, M.A., New Testament tutor at the Methodist College and already Special Lecturer in Hellenistic Greek at the University. Two full time lecturers were appointed and others added in succeeding years. It was also decided that some members of staff from Theological Colleges should be among the part-time lecturers invited to contribute their own subjects, as and when required by the Professor. Dr. Champion was designated Special Lecturer in New Testament and continued to provide classes in that subject and the Reverend Harry Mowvley, Special Lecturer in Hebrew, has been required to provide much of the teaching on the Old Testament. A course on Seventeenth Century Dissent became the responsibility of the Reverend Norman Moon, as a recognised teacher.

The changes in the University have affected the life of the College in various ways. Several of our students enter the University each year and they receive most of their academic teaching from University lecturers. They have as colleagues men and women preparing for a variety of careers, and belonging to churches of varied denominations. This has opened for them wider horizons intellectually, ecumenically and socially. By tutorials the College endeavours to assist its own undergraduates to relate their academic studies to the vocational.

Another effect has been to separate more widely our students reading for a degree from those preparing for the Diploma in Theology, since the classes are entirely separate. But smaller College classes have made possible different methods of teaching, by seminars, discussion groups, as well as lectures. Recently the College has switched from the London to the Cambridge

Diploma and Certificate in Theology.

The University Department has grown as the numbers of non-ministerial students has increased. At present (1978) there are over a hundred undergraduates, about thirty post-graduates. There are now two Professors, seven full-time lecturers and several part-time visiting lecturers. The syllabus[81] has been considerably widened, to offer a variety of options, and the opportunity for candidates to develop some specialisation in their final year. A wider range still has become possible through co-operation between departments in the Faculty of Arts. A few of our students have chosen to read for conjoint degrees in Theology and Sociology; Theology and English; Theology and Philosophy. Others who have graduated before entering our theological college have taken the Bristol post-graduate Diploma in Theology, leading to the M.A. One student has been awarded the M.Litt., for his thesis. These opportunities are particularly relevant to the needs of the growing number of those who respond to the call to the ministry after they have received a University education.

After twenty years as Principal of Western College, Dr. H. F. Lovell Cocks retired and was succeeded by the Reverend Basil H. Sims. Two years later in 1962, the Reverend W. J. Downes was succeeded as tutor by the Reverend Wilson Dennett. By 1968 the number of students at Western College had declined to around fourteen, and the Congregational Colleges at Nottingham, Bristol and Manchester decided to amalgamate at Manchester. This brought to a close the valuable co-operation between Western College and ourselves which had extended over sixty-five years. Generations of students had been enriched by sharing the insights of teachers from both Colleges.

The departure of Western College increased considerably the demands upon the three members of our staff, who were now required to cover the whole range of theological subjects for diploma courses, in addition to their commitments to the University Department of Theology.

Three Anglican Colleges in Bristol combined to form Trinity College, Bristol, and the Methodist Church amalgamated several Colleges, transferring much of their work to Wesley College, Bristol, as Didsbury College was re-named.

5. *Diversity of Students*

Although in 1918 the College agreed to accept women students, until 1960 only two women had taken advantage of this. From 1961 there began to be applications from women who felt called to the ministry, and one or two were accepted each year. Then in 1967 the Baptist Union asked if future candidates for the Order of Deaconesses could be trained in Bristol, instead of at Carey Hall, Birmingham. In the next three years, nine women joined the College community sharing classes with the men and entering fully into the life of the College. Miss Maud Townsend, a member of College Committee, was appointed Deaconess Tutor to give personal supervision to these women students. The extensions to the College provided a residential wing for women. In 1969 recruitment for the Order of Deaconesses ceased and in 1975 the Order was disbanded and the former deaconesses were placed on the ministerial list. A number of women continued to apply, some as ministerial candidates, some as 'open option' students. Several have entered the ministry, others have become teachers or social workers. Others have become ministers' wives! In the past decade the number of women students has averaged about seven, out of a total community of about forty. They have brought diversity into the College, socially, intellectually and spiritually.

More students came from overseas and made their own contributions in the Common Room and the Lecture Room. Three students came from the Soviet Union in 1956-1957. Others came from Bangladesh, Bhutan, Nagaland, Chile, Canada, Australia and Zaire. After completing their courses in Bristol, they returned to serve their own countries as ministers.

The age-range of students has progressively widened during the quarter of a century under review in this chapter. Previous generations of students entered College unmarried and most were in their early or middle twenties. A growing percentage of new candidates have been men in their late twenties or thirties, married, with young families. Most of these men were already established in their careers, several being graduates. College education has been made practicable by introducing them as student pastors to small churches. Here they preach

about two Sundays a month and through the vacations, and
give pastoral oversight, usually with the assistance of other
students. At present there are seven of these student ministries.
A number of churches have experienced new life and growth
and a few have been able to invite their student pastor to
become their full-time minister at the end of his course.[82]
While during term academic work has made heavy demands
on these students, they have benefited from the dovetailing of
pastoral training into practical experience.

6. The College and the Churches

In a variety of ways Dr. Champion developed opportunities
for the students to gain pastoral experience in the churches
during College days. It was his policy to strengthen the links
between the churches and the College. 'Open Day' and the
valedictory service at the end of the session, as well as the
Annual Meetings in October helped to achieve this. The work
of the College has depended on much more than the financial
support of the churches. It has required that people should
share the aims and ideals of the College, and seek out and
encourage gifted young people to recognise the claims of the
Christian ministry.

A new dimension was added to the College's work and
influence by the involvement of Dr. Champion in the affairs
of the Church Universal. Like his predecessors he was elected
President of the Baptist Union in 1964 when his Presidential
Address was on *The Resurrection of Christ*. To mark his election,
members of the College Committee and the Brotherhood
presented him with a portrait, painted by Mr. Walter Lambert.
It now hangs in the Lecture Room. In 1971 he was elected
Moderator of the Free Church Federal Council. More significant was his deep involvement in the work of the World
Council of Churches. He was Baptist delegate to the World
Council Assemblies at Evanston, New Delhi and Uppsala. He
was a member of its Faith and Order Commission from 1958
to 1972 and travelled widely, presenting the Baptist point of
view. With this first-hand knowledge of the World Church his
contribution as a Baptist to ecumenical thinking became highly
valued. In 1963 he published *Baptists and Unity* – one of a series
of denominational leaders. The position of Baptists was set

forth with clarity and conviction. For Dr. Champion the ecumenical movement helped to set Baptist principles in truer perspective.

His travels enabled him to visit Baptist Missionary Society stations in India and to lecture at Serampore, and meet some of his former students at work. In 1966 he visited the U.S.S.R., and again met his former students, now ministers in Moscow and in the Ukraine. Following his visit to India in 1966, he wrote in the College Report of the College's part in the foundation and the continued work of the Society and expressed his hope that 'God may continue to use the College to prepare his servants to go and make all nations disciples of Christ'. Altogether nine of Champion's men went overseas in the service of the Baptist Missionary Society to India, Bangladesh, Brazil and Zaire.

He retired from office in 1972. During his Principalship he met the changes of the age with flexibility of mind and clarity of purpose. Generations of students will pay their own tribute to his quiet firmness, his gentlemanly deportment, his vigorous mind, and his firm faith in Christ as Saviour and Lord.

Dr. Champion informed the College Committee in 1970 that he would be retiring in 1972. It so happened that Regent's Park were seeking a successor to Dr. G. Henton Davies at the same time and the two Committees agreed to keep in close contact in order to discover what was right for both Colleges seen together and to avoid any competition for one person. Two names clearly emerged, that of Dr. Morris West, for Bristol, and Dr. Barrington White, for Regent's Park.

7. Dr. Morris West Principal 1972-[83]

The Reverend W. M. S. West, M.A., D.Th., J.P., was appointed in 1971, working for one year with Dr. Champion, and commencing his Principalship in 1972. He is the son of the late Reverend W. E. West, himself a Bristol man in College at the turn of the century. Dr. West entered the College immediately after the Second World War under Dr. Dakin. He graduated in Bristol in 1949 and then in Oxford in 1951. He then went as Baptist Union Scholar to study at the University of Zurich, and presented a thesis on *John Hooper and the Origins of Puritanism* and was awarded a D.Th., in 1953. It had

been his firm intention to enter the pastoral ministry, but he
was persuaded to return to Regent's Park as Tutor in Church
History and remained there for six years. In 1959 he accepted
a call to the pastorate at St. Albans where he stayed until
1971. There his ministry was effective and widely appreciated.
He was appointed Justice of the Peace. He became deeply
involved in denominational affairs, serving especially as chairman of the Commission on the Associations, and in ecumenical
affairs as a member of the Faith and Order Commission of the
World Council of Churches. So he brought to Bristol his
academic ability, his teaching and pastoral experience, and his
knowledge of the World Church. Since his appointment he
has attended the Assembly of the World Council of Churches
in Nairobi in 1975, and meetings of the Faith and Order
Commission in different parts of the world. As chairman of the
Baptist Union Advisory Committee for Church Relations he
has been involved in defining the response of Baptists to the
'Ten Propositions' (1978). The Baptist Union elected him
President for the College's Tercentenary Year. In 1977 he
visited the U.S.S.R. and met some of those who had studied in
Bristol, and preached in their churches.

The University of Bristol appointed Dr. West as Special
Lecturer in Theology. He is particularly responsible for Reformation Studies. The six years of Dr. West's Principalship at
the College have continued to be years of orderly change.
Three years before Dr. Champion retired the College Committee had set up a 'policy group' to review the responses to
changes being made by the College. Their report suggested
guide lines to the new Principal. The reception of 'open
option' students was developed. This led to an increase in
numbers to forty-four in 1976. It resulted in the wider age-
range particularly because several ministerial students were
over thirty.[84]

The interviewing and assessment of new candidates has
taken on a new character. Under procedure agreed with the
Baptist Union, all ministerial applicants have first to be
interviewed and recommended by their local Baptist Association; the modern educational system provides academic tests,
which make a series of written examinations set by the College
irrelevant. Instead, the technique of a selection conference has

been developed, in which candidates are involved in group discussions with a member of staff. Each applicant in turn has a separate interview with members of staff and of the Committee. Thus when they appear before the full Candidates' Committee, several of its members have had some hours of personal contact on which to base their assessments.

8. Lay Training

One of the projects adopted in 1970 as part of the celebrations of the bi-centenary of the foundation of the Bristol Education Society was the development of the College as a resource centre for the education of lay folk. The L. G. Champion Fund raised over £20,000 to enable the College to extend its function in this way, and to provide a fourth full-time tutor. The programme has been varied: e.g., courses of lectures on about five successive Thursdays; weekend conferences on Fridays and Saturdays, affording fuller opportunity for group discussion; and involvement in projects. Reading or discussion groups have met over a period of months. One of these has brought together managers and trade unionists, members of our churches who have together tried to think through the Christian response to industrial problems. Another group produced a paper on 'Giving an account of the hope that is within us' – *Conversation about Hope* – which has been published in *Study Encounter*[85] by the World Council of Churches, and has been widely appreciated in many parts of the world.

The aim of the laity training courses has been to focus attention on areas of concern in modern life, and to relate theological thinking to the ethical, social and ecclesiastical issues. Groups of deacons from various churches have explored together the nature of their responsibilities. 'The teacher-pulpit relationship, a Christian concern' brought parents, teachers and ministers to share their insights. Courses of Bible Study have had a particular focus seeing 'Man Alive' in Biblical and in contemporary situations. 'Evangelism' included the specific task of Churches in inner areas of big cities, the problems facing these on new housing estates, and those in ecumenical areas of experiment. Such courses have brought together people with a specific concern, to share their thinking. Religious Liberty, the Multicultural Society, and the implications of the Assembly of the World Council, and British conversations about Church Unity have been explored under the guidance of specialist lecturers as well as members of the College staff. Some come to visit us from all parts of Britain. In Bristol itself there are men and women of considerable expertise and many significant social and religious enterprises, so that 'field-work' has been profitably integrated into the sessions held at the College.

The Extra-Mural Department of Bristol University has sponsored many of these courses; others have been planned in consultation with the Bristol Council of Churches. Each year about two hundred people, from churches in the West Country and the Midlands, have availed themselves of these opportunities. People from all major denominations, including bishops and Roman Catholic nuns, have participated.

Members of College staff, aided by students, have provided courses for groups of churches in Wiltshire, Somerset and Devon. Plans to extend to the Midlands are being worked out in partnership with Regent's Park College.

In 1972, the Reverend Keith Clements, M.A., then minister of Downend Baptist Church, Bristol, became Lay Training Organiser, on a part-time basis. The impact of this work and the widespread appreciation of it owes much to his imaginative leadership.

9. Pastoral Training

For several years the College recognised the need for a fourth full-time member of staff to share in the academic work, and more particularly to develop and co-ordinate the many aspects of pastoral training which had been introduced during the previous twenty years. Financial resources for such an extension of the College's ministry were provided partly from the L. G. Champion Fund and partly by the sale of a number of medieval manuscripts and a few printed Bibles from the Gifford Collection.

The Reverend Keith Clements was selected as the additional tutor, in 1977. He read Science and Theology at King's College, Cambridge, and then proceeded to Regent's Park College, Oxford, and graduated in Theology there in 1967. His main academic speciality is Theology in the 19th and 20th centuries, and in particular the theology of R. Gregor Smith. Baptist minister for ten years, first in the Mid-Cheshire Fellowship of Churches, then at Downend, Bristol, Clements was now called to help students to relate their pastoral experience and their theological thinking, and to explore with them further avenues of the Church's mission. This applies particularly to student pastors.

Through the whole span of the College's history, students have profited by observing the ministers in Bristol pulpits. Dr. Champion developed closer links through which students came to share in pastoral ministry of local churches. Now, those who are not student-pastors are each associated with a particular Bristol church for a year. Opportunity is given to sit in at deacon's meetings and at baptismal preparation classes, to share in pastoral visitation, and to observe the preparation and conduct of weddings and funerals. Thus under the guidance of an experienced minister the student is introduced to the responsibilities which lie ahead. Occasionally students not involved in University courses have been seconded to a church away from Bristol for two terms, during which time they are expected to continue their academic studies and send essays to their tutors. More extended experience is provided by a number of churches during summer vacations. Students usually spend a month under-studying the minister and then a month acting as his 'locum' during his holiday.

Particularly valuable are the carefully planned courses arranged by the Ministry of Health, which are shared by ordinands for the Anglican, Roman Catholic and Free Churches. Part of their time they work as orderlies on the wards. Special lectures and seminars are given by the medical staff and students are introduced to the methods of healing, to psychiatric clinics and to the work of the Hospital Chaplain. Such courses usually occupy a month of the summer vacation. In Bristol, the Department of Theology has arranged short courses in co-operation with the Department of Health. Other opportunities available during the summer include: experience in youth work provided by courses at Westhill College, Selly Oak, industrial experience, involving work on the factory floor; and seminars with the Industrial Chaplain.

Thus pastoral preparation ranging over a very wide area is available to the modern student, and while no one can be expected to have a taste of all, every student is required to devote part of each summer vacation to the broadening of his experience.

Within the College sermon class, speech training and classes in pastoral methods continue as of old, but with adaptations. In sermon workshop, a group of students and a tutor work out together a sermon on an agreed theme or text. A tutor sometimes visits a church to listen to a student conduct worship and preach.

Frequently, ministers, doctors and social workers are asked to contribute to the weekly pastoral theology class. Projects are organised involving study groups and 'field work' in Bristol on aspects of ministry such as the Family, Industrial relations, Industry, Religious Education.

All this, together with preaching on Sundays, makes heavy demands on a student's time and energy.

The policy of the College has always been to combine vocational training with academic work over the three or four years of a student's career. This is parallel to the procedure at Colleges of Education, in contrast to that favoured by Universities, where vocational training is concentrated into a postgraduate year. There is much value in a student absorbing insights into the ministerial task progressively as he or she matures in intellect and experience. The interspersing of theological study with practical experience is designed to encourage balanced growth. The primary task of a theological college is not merely to teach, certainly not to indoctrinate, nor merely to train in techniques, but to help students to grow *as persons*, as Christian men and women. For such a purpose the residential community is most valuable in itself. The provision of a tutor who can devote most of his attention to helping students to co-ordinate their theological thinking and their pastoral experiences has strengthened the College for its central purpose of education for ministry.

10. Other Baptist Colleges

Closer co-operation between the seven British Baptist Colleges has been worked out as the result of the report of an independent commission set up in 1973 to review the total situation of College training in Britain.

College staffs continue to meet annually in conference during each Easter vacation, and a wider fellowship exists with all our European Baptist tutors (including those from Eastern Europe), who meet approximately every three years. Recognising that Edward Terrill's vision and generosity inspired the beginning of the work of ministerial education is now continued in all our Colleges, Bristol has launched 'The Terrill Tercentenary Appeal' for a fund to endow bursaries for ministerial students who do not receive grants from their local Education Authorities. Students in all our seven British Colleges will be eligible to apply for help, through the Baptist Union Scholarships Committee.

Following a suggestion of the Commission on the Colleges that Cardiff and Bristol should consider working more closely, an interchange of lecturers has taken place for one day each week. Dr. West and the Reverend Norman Moon are now responsible for the Baptist share of teaching Church History at University College, Cardiff (University of Wales), while the Reverend Neville Clark[85] was appointed to the staff of South Wales Baptist College in 1975 in order also to supply the need for a New Testament lecturer at Bristol. The inter-change has worked well to the benefit of both Colleges. The relationship with Regent's Park College has continued. There are new opportunities for post-graduate courses.

The Baptist Union has developed a scheme to enable ministers to have sabbatical leave for a few months, every seven years. One room at Bristol has been set aside to accommodate any minister who wishes to spend a term here, and to assist him with his studies. A succession of such 'sabbaticals' has profited from study and contact with youthful students' minds; similarly our students have gained from the presence of these experienced ministers.

11. A Sense of Community[87]

During these years of change, every endeavour has been made to preserve the character of the College as a community in which students pray and work and study together, in common caring about the Church. The community has been enriched rather than divided by the diversity of age and sex, and by the presence of those doing Theology on open option. One third of students are not fully residential (chiefly the married men) but they share fully in student activities and in meals on weekdays. There is a sense of community not only in learning but in involvement with the work of the Kingdom, and especially in the ministry to the smaller Churches. 'Open option' students are not only full members of the College community, but are free, if they wish, to participate in all opportunities for vocational training and to serve on the 'preaching list'. Many choose to do this. It is significant that quite a high number of such students have 'opted' to become ministers during their College course. The ethos of the College remains that of a body of people devoted to the ministry of the Church.

From generation to generation the pattern of College life has been lectures in the morning, recreation in the afternoon and private study in the evenings. Diversity of lecture time-tables, including University classes in the afternoons, and the understandable wish of married students to work through the afternoon, and be free to spend their evenings with their families, has disturbed this pattern. The result has been a more flexible pattern of life, requiring of students personal self-discipline in planning their day.

Daily morning prayers bring together staff and students in the College Chapel, followed by a session for private devotions. Undoubtedly one of the most significant changes during the past decade has been the introduction of a service on Wednes-day evenings. Here the whole community, staff, students and their wives, meet for what has become a weekly Eucharist, conducted by students or staff, but frequently addressed by a visitor.

These acts of worship express the variety of religious and liturgical outlook within the community. Gifts of music and poetry have enriched the worship. The students have compiled their own book of prayers with liturgical responses, which is used from time to time. In 1978 a series of poems written by three of our students was published under the title *In Deeper Waters*.[87]

POSTSCRIPT

'By their fruits ye shall know them' is a test that applies to education societies as well as to individuals. Bristol Baptist College can be said fairly to match up to this criterion. Besides being the pioneer of Baptist Colleges throughout the world for the training of ministers, it has maintained the aims and standards set by its founders.

Some of its former students have gone on to become leaders of the Baptist denomination at home or abroad; others have become principals or tutors at Colleges; others again have served conspicuously in Baptist Missionary Society fields; a few have been called to specialised ministries in the communication of the Christian faith in industry, in schools, in broadcasting, in journalism, and in the social services. Most, however, have fulfilled their calling as pastors of local churches. So it is, that for three hundred years the College has endeavoured to remain faithful to its task of preparing able and evangelical ministers.

History is supposed to teach us lessons which we can apply to the present and the future. If this history teaches anything it is that the College has changed with the times but that its basic tasks and its underlying assumptions have remained the same. The sovereign grace of God, the centrality of Christ crucified and risen, the guidance and the power of the Holy Spirit – these do not change, and will not change. The Church, in some form or another, and the ministry in some form or another, will continue, and theological education will be needed for the whole Church. Consequently, the institution which Edward Terrill envisaged in 1679 for the education of ministers must continue to change and may even cease to be, but the tasks which it has sought to fulfil and the truths of the Gospel which it has taught will abide.

COLLEGE CHAPEL

STUDENTS AND STAFF 1978

Bibliography

No official records exist of the period before the foundation of the Bristol Education Society in 1770. Since then there have been manuscript minutes and the annual printed reports. The manuscript minutes of Broadmead Baptist Church, of which Isaac James (*1775) made extensive transcripts, contain considerable information of the earlier period.

C. S. Hall (*1929) has compiled a card index of all Bristol College students, giving biographical and bibliographical details. This, and fuller notes, are available at the College.

Abbreviations

*   Indicates year of entry as a student at Bristol.

Rippon: *A.R.*
John Rippon, D.D. (*1771). *A Brief Essay toward a history of the Academy at Bristol* (1796). A lecture given to the Bristol Education Society, 26th August, 1795. This is reproduced in Rippon's *Annual Register*, Vol. II, pp. 413-456.
Original MS. at Dr. Williams' Library.

Swaine
S. A. Swaine (*1869). *Faithful Men, or Memorials of Bristol Baptist College* (1884). A full account of the College to the year 1868 with biographical notes on some of the men educated in the College.
A. G. Hamlin (*1911). MS. continues Swaine to 1922 (in College Library).

Trestrail
F. Trestrail (*1828). *Reminiscences of College Life in Bristol.* Period 1828-1831.

Abbreviations (continued)

Hawker

> G. Hawker (*1873): *Records and Reminiscences* (1922). Period 1868-1922.
>
> Robertson Nicoll, 'Our Debt to Bristol Baptist College', *British Weekly*, 1910.
>
> L. G. Champion (*1926), N. S. Moon (*1935) and H. Mowvley (*1946): *The Bristol Education Society, 1770-1970* (1970).
>
> F. E. Robinson (*1884). 'Bristol Baptist College – the 250th Anniversary'. *B.Q.* IV No. 7. July 1929, pp. 292-299.
>
> A. Dakin. *Bristol Baptist College – 250 years 1679-1929* (1929).

Foreman

> Henry Foreman. *The Early Separatists, The Baptists and Education*, 1580-1780. *With special reference to the education of the Clergy*. Thesis for Ph.D., of Leeds University, 1976, part of which is published in the *Baptist Quarterly*, Vol. XXVII (1978), pp. 358-369. 'Baptist Provision for Ministerial Education in the Eighteenth Century'. Gives detailed consideration to Bristol College; also *Journal* of Educational Administration and History, Vol. X No. 1, January 1978. 'A Sixteenth Century Radical's Views on Education; Henry Barrow'.

B.Q.

> *Baptist Quarterly.*

B.M.

> *Baptist Magazine.*

B.R.

> *Broadmead Records* (see Note 1).

D.N.B.

> *Dictionary of National Biography.*

Notes

[1] EDWARD TERRILL AND BROADMEAD BAPTIST CHURCH (founded 1640). See *The Records of a Church of Christ in Bristol, 1640-1687,* ed. Roger Hayden (*1959), Bristol Record Society Vol. XXVII (1974). Earlier editions: by E. B. Underhill (1847), and N. Haycroft (1865).

EDWARD TERRILL (1634-*c*.1685) was born at Almondsbury, Gloucestershire, brought to Bristol by his mother in 1640, and was apprenticed as a scrivener. He worked as a 'writing schoolmaster' and became involved in the sugar trade developing between Bristol and the West Indies. He also inherited wealth by his marriage to William Listun's daughter (Dorothy Heath) in 1668. Underhill (pp. 57-59) inserted Terrill's own account of his religious experience from 1654. He was involved in the sufferings of the Church, was imprisoned, and fined several times under the Conventicle Act. Using material from others for the years 1640-1654, Terrill wrote *The Broadmead Records* until his own death.

EDWARD TERRILL'S CHARITY
T. J. Manchee: *Bristol Charities,* Vol. I (1831), pp. 280-284. R. Hayden summarises (*B.R.* 10-11). 'There is no way of establishing exactly when Terrill died, but it is known that on 7th January 1685/6 his wife married Thomas Vaux, the subsequent pastor of Broadmead. *Bristol Charities* gives the details of the considerable estates which Terrill left to the church and for the provision of an educated ministry. There were six acres called Culver Close, near Maudlin Lane; a paddock called Puckingrove, beyond Red Lodge on the way to Clifton; two houses with stables and gardens just outside Lawford's Gate, plus four acres of ground in the King's Marsh, Barton Regis; the "Three Pigeons" at the Quay Head, and the house opposite; a house in Baldwin Street; three houses on Michael's Hill. The property was to be used "for the congre-

gation of which Edward Terrill was a member and Thomas
Hardcastle was pastor". The money was delegated in various
ways. Ten poor people were to receive a sum following Terrill's
death, and the remainder was to be administered "for the
subsistence of a holy, learned, man, well skilled in the tongues,
to wit Greek and Hebrew, and should profess and practice the
truth of believers baptism as a pastor or teacher to the congregation aforesaid, as to another, after his death successively
forever". There was also a provision for paying £10 per year,
for a maximum of four years, to poor Baptist students. He
also left money to the poor at Almondsbury, where he had
lived with his aunt, and something for Thomas Hardcastle's
daughter, "Prisona alias Mary". The provisions for the
Broadmead chapel and the training of Baptist ministers came
into effect when Robert Bodenham established a trust fund in
1715 to make Terrill's wishes an effective reality.'

Terrill's will is dated 25th September 1683 (P.C.C. 1685).
He bequeathed his library to Broadmead. It contained works
in English, Greek, Hebrew and Latin.

[2] BROADMEAD MINISTERS (*B.R.* 17-46).

THOMAS EWINS (1617-1670) first served as Bristol City Lecturer,
then, after his ejection in 1660, he was ordained as Broadmead's
first minister, serving until his death in 1670. 'Though he had
not ye Originall tongues, yett God did indue him with greate
grace and quick understanding in ye things of God and ye
Gospel . . .' (*B.R.* 127).

THOMAS HARDCASTLE (1636-1678), graduated at Cambridge, was
Vicar of Bramham, near Leeds, until ejected, 1660. He was
imprisoned seven times, five times during his ministry at
Broadmead, 1671-1678.
Broadmead then invited Robert Browne, an Oxford graduate
minister at Westmancote, but his church declined to release
him. A month later Terrill made his deed of gift to provide for
an educated ministry.

GEORGE FOWNES (d. 1685), educated at Emmanuel College,
Cambridge, he became Vicar at High Wycombe, but resigned
before the Restoration. Ministered at Broadmead from 1679
until his death in Gloucester gaol, where he had spent nearly
three years.

[3] BAPTISTS AND MINISTERIAL EDUCATION IN THE 17TH CENTURY.

Thomas Collier: *The Pulpit Guard Routed* (1652), p. 25.

J. Rippon: *A.R.* II, pp. 418-419.

N. S. Moon: 'Caleb Evans, Founder of Bristol Education Society', *B.Q.* XXIV (1971), pp. 179-182.

H. Foreman. *op. cit.* (Thesis — *passim*)

R. E. Cooper: *From Stepney to St. Giles* (1960), pp. 14-20.

James Ivimey: *History of English Baptists*, Vol. I, pp. 415-420.

These review the various attitudes of Baptists to the question of education for the Baptist ministry.

⁴ Pithay Church, Bristol (*B.R.* 70-71). Founded *c.* 1650. The first minister, Henry Hynam, was succeeded in 1679 by Andrew Gifford, who, like many of his successors was closely involved with Broadmead in its work of educating ministers.

J. G. Fuller: *Dissent in Bristol* (1840), pp. 215-252.

⁵ William Thomas (d. 1693), was an Oxford graduate, a minister and schoolmaster, ejected in 1660, probably not a Baptist. 'E. Calamy (Revised)' III, p. 482, says 'he trained up many for the ministry'.

Richard Sampson became minister at Exeter 1692-1716.

⁶ Other Bequests to Broadmead.

Robert Bodenham (d. 1726), was a member of Broadmead, and involved with Terrill in his business. By deed of 13th January, 1715, he stipulated that certain properties were to be vested in Broadmead 'for the maintenance support and education, from time to time, of such young men for the ministry of the Gospel'. By the end of the eighteenth century, it was calculated, the annual rental from these properties, to the College, amounted to £60 10s., while those in support of the Broadmead minister amounted to £70. By a second indenture, dated 27th August, 1720, Bodenham gave a newly erected house and buildings in Broadmead to the Church for 'the use of Bernard Foskett and others, their heirs and assigns, for ever'.

By deed of gift dated 16th March, 1728, Bernard Foskett gave £160 for the rebuilding of these houses adjacent to the Church. (They were rebuilt in 1780.)

Dorothy Vaux (formerly Terrill), bequeathed £100 in 1695 for the support of the Broadmead minister, and a further £100, the interest being 'for the educating young brethren in the tongues in which the Scriptures were written in order to their help in the ministry, for ever'.

Sir John Eyles, likewise bequeathed £100 'to be applied for the educating of young persons and making them fit for the ministry.'

Manchee, *op.cit.*, pp. 275-301. W. Sherring, *Bristol Baptist Fund* (1884), p. 23. Dr. H. Foreman, comments on this generous provision for the support of the ministry at Broadmead: 'Irrespective of any payment which the members of Broadmead might make him, the minister was assured, by the end of the eighteenth century, of £75 per annum and free accommodation. Through the foresight and care of its founders, the Bristol Baptist College had been provided with a sound basis upon which its work could be built and founded.' This he contrasts with the situation among London Baptists at that time. See: Foreman: *B.Q.* Vol. XXVII (1978), pp. 358-361.

In 1870, these gifts to Broadmead were incorporated into the Terrill Foskett Trust and the income is divided between the College and the Church. The capital is currently valued at £30,000 and the College receives about £1,200 annually. Trustees are appointed by the Church and by the College.

[7] TROWBRIDGE ACADEMY: TEWKESBURY ACADEMY: see note 15.

[8] BERNARD FOSKETT (1685-1758). Younger son of William Foskett, of North Crawley, Buckinghamshire, 'a gentleman of good repute, easy fortune and blessed with a numerous offspring'. Bernard was born at Woburn, Bedfordshire, on 10th March, 1685, and received a private education. Made considerable progress in several branches of knowledge, including medicine (see F. Essex Lewis, 'Broadmead Records', *B.Q.* X (1940), p. 224. Member of Little Wild Street Church, London, under the ministry of John Pigott. Co-pastor with John Beddome of group of churches at Henley-in-Arden, Bengeworth (Evesham) and Alcester 1711-1720. Beddome followed Foskett to Bristol in 1724, becoming minister of Pithay Church. Hugh Evans' tribute to Foskett is included in a footnote to the printed sermon by Caleb Evans on the death of his father: *Elisha's Exclamation* (1781), pp. 22-27. MS. in Hugh Evans' own hand is in Dr. Williams's Library.

[9] THE PARTICULAR BAPTIST FUND (The 'London Fund'), was established by six churches in London in 1717 for the assistance of ministers, and to assist the education of future ministers. It assisted Baptists studying at Dissenting Academies (see note 15).

T. F. Valentine: *Concern for the Ministry* (1967).

THE BRISTOL BAPTIST FUND was also established in 1717 'in order to make provision for the support of and succession in the

Baptist Ministry'. It made grants to individual students studying at various academies, and particularly in Bristol College.
Since 1843 it has voted a block grant to the College, and to its
library (£650 in 1978).
W. Sherring: *Bristol Baptist Fund* (1884); A. J. Betteridge:
Bristol Baptist Fund (1958).
Bristol Students were sponsored by both these funds until 1812,
when with the founding of Stepney College it was decided that
the Bristol Baptist Fund should apply to ministers and students
in the West Country, and the Particular Baptist Fund to the
rest of Britain.

[10] ANDREW GIFFORD (Junior), (1700-1784).
L. G. Champion, *Farthing Rushlight* (1961), pp. 31-34. See note
27.

[11] HUGH EVANS (1713-1781). Second son of Caleb Evans, Baptist
minister in Radnorshire, and grandson of Thomas Evans of
Pentre. Hugh was educated under Richard Pryce, minister at
Llwynllwyd, from whom he received a good grounding in
classical studies.
Caleb Evans: *Elisha's Exclamation* (1781), for funeral tribute;
N. S. Moon: 'Caleb Evans', *B.Q.* XXIV (1971), pp. 175-176.

[12] MINISTERS' HOUSES
The houses, numbers 1 and 2 North Street, situated nearly
opposite the Full Moon in Stokes Croft were by indenture of
23rd October, 1745, vested in Broadmead for the benefit of
Bernard Foskett and Hugh Evans during their ministry, and
thereafter to their successors. By the will of Henry Ramsey, a
deacon of Broadmead, who died on 19th July, 1761, these
houses were secured for the ministers 'for their own use while
they served this Church, and for the use of their successors . . .
to be considered no part of their salary, but to render them
the more easy and comfortable'. T. J. Manchee, *op.cit.*, pp.
288-289.

[13] JOHN COLLETT RYLAND (1723-1792)
His diary is reproduced from the MS. in the Angus Library at
Regent's Park College, in *B.Q.* Vol. II, pp. 249-252. 'A
Student's Programme in 1744'. H. Wheeler Robinson: 'A
Baptist Student – John Collett Ryland', *The Life and Faith of
the Baptists* (1927), pp. 60-73. *B.Q.* III, pp. 25-33. Barbara
Wright: 'John Collet Ryland (1723-1792) Baptist Minister,
Schoolmaster and Writer' (unpublished thesis; copy with

author). J. C. Culross: *The Three Rylands* (1897). *D.N.B.* XVII,
p. 545.

[14] FOSKETT'S LECTURES

Two MSS. of his lecture notes on 'Pneumatology' are preserved
at the College. Volume I was transcribed by Benjamin Beddome
and presented to the College in 1794. It deals with philosophical subjects: the soul, psychology, angels, good and evil.
Volume II was presented by Dr. Andrew Gifford in 1780 and
includes Psychology, Philosophy and Physiology – the anatomy
of the mind (was Foskett using his medical studies?), as well
as Theism, 'The nature, government and attributes of the
Supreme Mind as far as is discoverable'. The manuscript adds
several sciences founded on the knowledge of the human mind,
viz. Logic, Music, Ethics and Politics.

H. McLachlan: *English Education under the Test Acts* (1931),
p. 276; cf. Philip Doddridge: *Works*, Vol. IV (1804), pp. 298 ff.

[15] DISSENTING ACADEMIES

The following books on the Dissenting Academies review the
contribution of Bristol Baptist College.

H. McLachlan: *English Education under the Test Acts* (1931);
Irene Parker: *Dissenting Academies in England* (1914); J. W.
Ashley Smith: *The Birth of Modern Education* (1954); H. Foreman: 'When it is borne in mind that J. C. Ryland's course
may have been only two years of duration as against four of
Doddridge's and that Bristol was solely concerned with training ministers, the work of Bristol does not compare unfavourably with that of institutions such as Kibworth' (where
Philip Doddridge was a student).

S. J. Price: 'Dissenting Academies 1662-1820'. *B.Q.* VI (1932),
pp. 125-138.

V. Murray: 'Doddridge and Education'. Chapter V in *Philip
Doddridge (1702-1751), His Contribution to English Religion*;
edited by G. F. Nuttall (1951).

G. F. Nuttall: *New College, London and its Library*; 'Friends of
Dr. William's Library (1977); 'The Students of Trevecca
College'. *Transactions* of Cymmrodorion Society (1967), pp.
249-277.

S. G. Harries: 'The Status of Doddridge's Academy'. Transactions of Congregational Historical Society XVII (1952),
pp. 19-25.

TROWBRIDGE ACADEMY

Ashley Smith, *op.cit.*, pp. 91-92, 198.

Victoria County History of Wiltshire, Vol. VII (1953), p. 158.
cf. *B.Q.* VI (1932), p. 135.

TEWKESBURY ACADEMY
McLachlan, *op. cit.* pp. 126-131; Irene Parker, *op. cit.* pp. 96-101.

[16] WESTERN COLLEGE was founded at Ottery St. Mary in 1752, and
had had various homes in the West Country: Bridport,
Taunton, Axminster, Exeter and was at Plymouth 1845-1901,
when it moved to Cotham, Bristol. In 1968 it amalgamated
with other Congregational Colleges at Manchester.
McLachlan, *op.cit.*, pp. 3-4, 12. J. Charteris Johnston 'Western
College' in *Transactions* of Congregational Historical Society
Vol. VII (1916), pp. 98-131; see further Chapters V and VI.

[17] STUDENTS UNDER FOSKETT
Dr. Rippon (*A.R.* II, p. 428), said that there were sixty-four
students, thirty-two from England and thirty-two from Wales.
This list has been checked against the MSS. of Joshua Thomas,
and the list of students from Wales between 1720 and 1797 is
to be published by Dr. G. F. Nuttall in *Transactions* of the
Cymmrodorion Society (1979). See note 28. In addition to
those mentioned in the text, Dr. Rippon also singles out
Robert Day (Wellington), John Evans (Northampton), John
Evans (Pentre), John Oulton (Rawdon), Dr. Morgan Jones
(Hammersmith), Edmund Watkins (Usk).

[18] BENJAMIN BEDDOME, M.A. (1707-1795) *1737. Minister at
Bourton-on-the-Water 1740-1795.

Thomas Brooks: *Pictures of the Past* (1861), pp. 21-60; Rippon:
A.R. II, pp. 314-317; III pp. 415-421; also see notes 19 and
30.

JOHN ASH, LL.D.(Edin) (1724-1779), *1740. Minister at Pershore
1751-1779.
Published: *Sentiments on Education* (1777); *New and Complete
Dictionary of the English Language* (1775, 2nd ed. 1795); *Grammatical Institutes, or an easy introduction to Lowth's English Grammar*
(1766). Hymns (see note 19).

G. H. Taylor: 'The Reverend John Ash'. *B.Q.* XX (1963),
pp. 4-22.
G. F. Nuttall: 'John Ash and the Pershore Church'. *B.Q.* XXII
(1968), pp. 271-276.
Caleb Evans: *Funeral Sermon* (1779).
D.N.B. Vol. I, p. 633.

BENJAMIN FRANCIS, M.A. (1734-1799) *1753. Minister at Horsley (Nailsworth), Glos. 1758-1799.
Wrote Hymns and Elegies (see note 19).

Wm. Winterbotham: *History of Baptised Church at Shortwood* (1820).

G. F. Nuttall: 'Questions and Answers', *B.Q.* XXVII (1977), pp. 83-89.

Joshua Thomas: *History of the Baptist Churches in Wales* (see note 28).

[19] HYMNODY

We are indebted to the Reverend Eric Sharpe for his article, 'Bristol Baptist College and the Church's Hymnody', *B.Q.* Vol. XXVIII, January 1979.

EDMUND JONES (*1738), who introduced hymns to his Church at Exeter, wrote *Sacred Poems* (1760).

JOHN ASH (*1740) and CALEB EVANS. *Collection of Hymns adapted to Public Worship* (1769), contained 412 hymns including those of Watts, Wesley and Doddridge. Hitherto congregations had depended on the published hymns of Watts and on 'lining out' of works by composers.

JOSEPH KINGHORN (*1784) bought copies of the *Collection* for use by his choir at Norwich, and he published special editions with supplements in 1814 and 1827.

BENJAMIN BEDDOME (*1737)
Wrote 830 hymns, thirteen were included in collections by Ash and Evans, and thirty-six in Rippon's *Selections*. All were published in *Hymns of the late B. Beddome, M.A.* (1817), with preface by Robert Hall.

BENJAMIN FRANCIS (*1753) wrote hymns and elegies.
Five were included in Rippon's *Selection*. *Baptist Hymn Book* (1962), No. 293 is his revision of a hymn by Joseph Grigg. He composed nearly two hundred hymns in Welsh, published in two volumes in 1774 and 1786, of which fifteen are included in *Y Llawlyfr Moliant Newydd* (1956).

JOHN RIPPON (*1769). *A Selection of Hymns from the Best Authors* was intended as an appendix to Watts' *Psalms and Hymns* (1787). The final edition (1844) *The Comprehensive Rippon* contained 1,200 hymns. Rippon's first tune book was published in 1791, 7th edition (1815) known as *Walker's Companion*. Rippon wrote an Oratorio, *The Crucifixion* (published 1837).

SAMUEL PEARCE (*1786) wrote hymns and poems which are included in A. Fuller, *Memoirs of Samuel Pearce* (1800).

JOHN RYLAND was writing hymns at the age of sixteen, 36 of which are in his *Serious Essays* (1771). Later hymns are in his *Pastoral Memorials* (1828), Vol. 2, pp. 423/448.

THOMAS THOMAS (*1777) wrote hymns and elegies in Welsh.

JOSEPH HARRIS (*1804) used name 'Gomer', wrote several hymns. He published a volume of 800 hymns for use of Welsh Baptists (1821).

J. H. HINTON (*1811) wrote many hymns.

JOHN EUSTACE GILES (*1826) wrote several hymns, several on missionary themes, one of which was a hymn in celebration of the emancipation of slaves.

MAURICE HEWETT (*1907) wrote a number of hymns and published them in *Brookfield Hymns* (1940).

KEITH CLEMENTS now a tutor at the College contributed to *Praise for Today* (1974). Hymn No. 17.

The Baptist Hymn Book (1952), includes two hymns by Beddome – 'Witness ye men and angels now' (No. 304), and 'Father of Mercies' (No. 364); and John Ryland's 'Let us sing the King Messiah' (No. 377).

Other Bristol contributions are –
'Jesus and shall it ever be' (No. 293), which is a revision of the work of Joseph Grigg by Benjamin Francis; 'All hail the power of Jesus' name' (No. 180), by Edward Perronet, revised by John Rippon; and Joshua Marshman's translation of the hymn by Krishna Pal, Carey's first convert from Hinduism, 'O Thou my Soul' (No. 213). See *The Baptist Hymn Book Companion* (1962).

[20] THOMAS LLEWELYN, LL.D.(Aberdeen) (1720-1783), was born at Penallton, Glamorgan. Educated at Trosnant Academy, then Bristol College in 1741-1743, and then at Dr. Jennings' Academy in London. In 1752 he formed 'a Baptist Society for assisting young men in Grammar and Academic Learning', stressing the Study of the Bible in the original languages (see *B.Q.* IX (1939), p. 422; *B.T.* VI (1918), p. 114. (Minutes in Angus Library, Regent's Park College, Oxford.)
Caleb Evans referred to Llewelyn as 'the most complete scholar and gentleman'. Dr. Gibbons – 'Dr. Llewelyn has more classical learning than any minister among Baptists'. Aberdeen

University awarded him the M.A., and LL.D. He was one of
the first members of the Cymmrodorion Society, and President
in 1775. He was influential in the widest circulation of the
Welsh Bible, published by the S.P.C.K. in 1769. See *Dictionary
of Welsh Biography*, p. 568, *D.N.B.* XI, p. 1286.

In 1776 he took a prominent part in the establishment of a
Baptist Mission to North Wales, see note 31 (*B.Q.* X, p. 123).
Rippon, *A.R.* I, pp. 183-185.

[21] MORGAN EDWARDS (1722-1795), was born at Trevethin, Monmouthshire. A member at Pen-y-garn, went to Trosnant
Academy, and thence to Bristol in 1742. After three pastorates
in Britain, he went to Philadelphia as minister, 1761-1771.
Was a strong Royalist during the American war. Historian of
the Baptists in Pennsylvania. He founded the Baptist College,
Rhode Island (now Brown University). Although the President
of the College was to be a Baptist, all other positions on the
staff were to be open to all denominations 'to enjoy full, free,
absolute and uninterrupted liberty of conscience'.

D. M. HIMBURY. 'Training Baptist Ministers', *B.Q.* XXI (1966),
pp. 345-346. Rhode Island College conferred honorary degrees
on several British Baptists, see Rippon *A.R.* II, pp. 308-314;
B.Q. X, p. 123. Among these were the following Bristol principals and students:

D.D. – John Rippon, John Ryland, Caleb Evans.

M.A. – Thomas Dunscombe, John Fawcett, Benjamin Francis,
J. C. Ryland.

See also: Robert Kenny, *Town and Gown in Wartime* (1976);
Roger Hayden, unpublished thesis on 'William Staughton;
Baptist Educator, Missionary, Educator and Pastor' (1965),
pp. 34-48.

[22] CALEB EVANS, D.D. (1737-1791)

Son of Hugh and Sarah Evans. Never a formal student at this
College. Educated at Mile End Academy, London, under Dr.
Walker, Dr. Gibbons and Dr. Conder. Assistant minister at
Unicorn, Yard Church, Southwark, and then at Clapham,
London (1757-1758). Broadmead called him to assist his father
– December 1758. Married Sarah Jeffries 1762 who died 1771.
Married Sarah Hazel, 1774. Died 9th August, 1791.

Funeral Sermons by Samuel Stennett and John Tommas.
See also *Baptist Magazine* 1817, p. 321.

Benjamin Francis: *Elegy on Death of Caleb Evans*. Rippon:

A.R. I, pp. 247-252. N. S. Moon, *B.Q.* XXIV, pp. 175-190.
See further notes 19, 30 and 32.
Publications: E. Starr, *Baptist Bibliography*, Vol. 7, pp. 99-104
lists 73 of his publications.

[23] Caleb Evans's Address to Students 1770, and his list of recommended books is reproduced in Rippon *A.R.* I, pp. 345-351,
253-256, also in Swaine, pp. 126-133.

[24] BRISTOL EDUCATION SOCIETY
Swaine: pp. 70-79. See Appendix A.

[25] JAMES NEWTON (1734-1790)
Rippon: *A.R.* I, pp. 150-154, 563.
Funeral Sermon, by Caleb Evans and John Tommas (1790).

[26] ANNUAL SERMONS
From 1773 onwards a preacher was appointed to address the
students at the Annual Meeting of the Society. These sermons
were printed from 1773. The first sermon was preached by
Hugh Evans – *The Able Minister* based on 2 Corinthians 3: 6,
in which he argued for the compatibility of reliance on the
Holy Spirit, and on human learning.

[27] THE LIBRARY
Andrew Gifford (see note 10). Minister at Little Wild Street,
Church, London, and then at Eagle Street, London (1730-
1784). His will (1782) stated:
'Whereas I have been earnestly requested not to destroy my
manuscripts as I thought, I hereby desire that the said
Messrs. Ryland and Robinson will look over them and
preserve those which they shall think proper (and destroy
the rest) which I hereby give and bequeath to the Society
of Baptists in Bristol for the education of young men for the
ministry, which said MSS. together with my books, my
pictures, also my curiosities, natural history and the rest of
my museum I hereby give to the aforesaid Baptist Academy
and Museum at Bristol.'
L. G. Champion: *Farthing Rushlight* (1961), pp. 85-95; Mac-
Lachlan (*op.cit.*, pp. 100-101) lists some of the scientific
apparatus included in the catalogue of the College Library
(1795). See also Swaine, pp. 343-368.

[28] LINKS WITH WALES
We are much indebted to Reverend Dr. Geoffrey Nuttall for
his lecture to the Honourable Society of Cymmrodorion in

London on 7th February, 1978, entitled 'Welsh Students at Bristol Baptist College, 1720-1797'. This is to be published in their *Transactions* in 1979. From the editions of Joshua Thomas of 1778 and 1885 Dr. Nuttall has identified eighty-seven Welsh students who studied at Bristol and added the names of three others. Bristol College possesses the manuscripts of Joshua Thomas, 'Materials for a History of the Baptist Churches of Wales' (1782) and 'History of the Baptist Churches in Wales' (1795).

[29] TROSNANT ACADEMY

D. Mervyn Himbury: *South Wales Baptist College* (1957), pp. 11-14; T. M. Bassett: *The Welsh Baptists* (1977), pp. 68-69; Selwyn Gummer: *Trosnant Academy, B.Q.* IX (1939), pp. 417-424; Joshua Thomas: 'History of the Baptist Churches in Wales', MS., pp. 320-329.

[30] EVANGELICAL CALVINISM

See notes on Hugh and Caleb Evans, and especially the latter's *Confession of Faith*, delivered at his ordination (1767) and other published works.   cf. N. S. Moon, *B.Q.* XVIV (1971), pp. 176-178.

'Western Association', Somerset Confession, 1656.

W. L. Lumpkin, *The Baptist Confessions of Faith* (1969), pp. 210-216.

Western Association Letter, 1769 (by Caleb Evans), p. 5.

Bristol Students who exemplify this outlook were:

Benjamin Beddome (*1737). Rippon: *A.R.* II (1795), p. 321.

John Ash (*1740). Sermon to Bristol Education Society – *The Perfecting of the Saints* (1778), pp. 8-13.

Benjamin Francis (*1753). Thomas Flint: *Sketch of the Life of Benjamin Francis* (1799), pp. 60-62.

John Rippon (*1769). K. Manley: 'The Making of an Evangelical Baptist Leader', *B.Q.* XXVI (1976), pp. 254-274.

John Sutcliff (*1772). A. Fuller: *Funeral Sermon for Sutcliff* (1814): Fuller's Works, Vol. IV (1837), pp. 325-334. K. Howard: 'John Sutcliff of Olney', *B.Q.* XIV (1952), p. 308.

Joseph Kinghorn (*1784). M. H. Wilkin: *Joseph Kinghorn of Norwich* (1856), pp. 175-177 – Kinghorn's Ordination Statement.

Samuel Pearce (*1786). A. Fuller: *Memoirs of Samuel Pearce, Works* (1837), Vol. V, pp. 85-110.

Robert Hall (*1778) moved further from Calvinism but repudiated the suggestion he was tending towards Unitarianism. Gregory Olinthus: 'Memoir' in Robert Hall's *Works*, Vol. VI (1832), pp. 26-30. See note 33.

Bristol Students who moved further from the Calvinist position included Job David (*1768), who became a Unitarian; John Evans (*1783), who became a General Baptist; William Richards (*1773).

J. A. Oddy: 'The Dissidence of William Richards', *B.Q.*. Vol. XXVII (1977), pp. 118-127.
John Evans: *Memoirs of William Richards* (1819).
Hugh Evans wrote to Richards in 1778 – 'I have thought that there is great wisdom and goodness in our not seeing all alike as is our having different faces and dispositions' (p. 43).

Others who became Unitarians were:
Anthony Robinson (*1784), Robert Aspland (*1798) and Thomas Southwood Smith (*1803).
F. N. L. Poynter: 'Thomas Southwood Smith – the man' (1788-1861). '*Proceedings* of the Royal Society of Medicine', Vol. 55, pp. 381-392, Poynter describes how Smith changed his theological views and then left Bristol College to study medicine at Edinburgh, and became influential in the realm of Sanitary Reform.

[31] SUMMER MISSIONS
From 1773 onwards the Bristol Education Society voted funds to enable students to share in itinerant missions in Cornwall, work sponsored by the B.M.S. For the report for 1797 by Saffery and William Steadman (*1789) see Rippon, *A.R.* II, pp. 459-464, III, pp. 56-59. Bristol Students looked after their churches while Saffery and Steadman were away. Likewise Bristol students shared in the mission to North Wales, inspired by Thomas Llewelyn in 1776. T. M. Bassett, *op.cit.*, pp. 100-106.

[32] SOCIAL AND POLITICAL CONCERN
Hugh Evans: *Ministers described under the characters of Fathers and Prophets* (1773).
T. M. Bassett: *op.cit.*, pp. 99-122.
Caleb Evans: *Sermon on Constitutional Liberty* (1775); *Letter to the Reverend Mr. John Wesley* (1775); *British Freedom Realised* (1788).
James Dore (*1779): *On the African Slave Trade* (1788).
Thomas Langdon (*1778): *Memoir of Thomas Langdon by his daughter* (1837).

Isaiah Birt (*1780): 'Memoir', *B.M.* 1838, p. 54.

S. Pearce Carey: *Samuel Pearce.*

Morgan John Rhys (*1786), *D.N.B.* XVI, p. 968.

William Richards (*1775) (see note 30).

R. T. Jenkins: 'William Richards of Kings Lynn. *Transactions* Welsh Baptist Historical Society' (1930) emphasises that America was the political and spiritual home of Wm. Richards and Morgan Rhys. It was from America, not from France, that they gained their radical views.

³³ ROBERT HALL (1764-1831) *1778

Son of Robert Hall, who ministered at Arnsby, Leicestershire. Classical Tutor 1785-1791. See further note 51.

³⁴ JOSEPH KINGHORN (1766-1832) *1784

M. H. Wilkins: *Joseph Kinghorn of Norwich* (1855), pp. 69-114, reproduces Kinghorn's letters from Bristol describing College life. See also notes 19 and 30.

³⁵ JOSEPH HUGHES (1769-1833) *1784

In July, 1791, Broadmead 'at the request of Dr. Evans, our Pastor, became a temporary assistant to him in the ministry and the Academy'. The invitation was confirmed (not unanimously) by the Church, in December. He continued to serve as Tutor during the interregnum, and then with Dr. Ryland until July 1796.

J. Leifchild: *Memoir of Joseph Hughes* (1835).

³⁶ DR. WARD'S TRUST

By an indenture dated 1754, John Ward left £1,200 stock to endow the education of two young men, sons of Dissenters (preferably Baptists) at some University in Scotland (preferably Edinburgh).

John Ward, the son of a Baptist minister, was Professor of Rhetoric at Gresham College, London.

Most of the 18th century Ward Scholars went to Aberdeen, e.g., Robert Hall and Joseph Hughes. After 1806, Edinburgh and Glasgow were more favoured. Altogether twenty of Ryland's students proceeded to Scotland for further study followed by a similar number of Crisp's students. About half of these men were supported by the Dr. Ward Trust, others were financed by their fathers, and a few by the Bristol Education Society or the Bristol Baptist Fund. John Mack was paid for by the Serampore Missionaries.

E. J. Tongue (*1900): *Dr. John Ward's Trust* (1951) (*B.Q.* 1950-1951, Vol. XIII-XIV). On page 14 the first Ward Scholar is noted as Caleb Evans. He was the cousin of Dr. Caleb Evans, who became Principal of Bristol College.

[37] WILLIAM STAUGHTON (1770-1829) *1791

S. W. Lynd: *A Memoir of the Reverend William Staughton, D.D.* Boston 1834.

Roger Hayden (*1959): 'William Staughton: Baptist Educator, Missionary Advocate and Pastor'; an unpublished thesis, in the College Library. See also his articles: 'Kettering 1792 and Philadelphia 1814'; *B.Q.* Vol. XXI (1965), pp. 3-19, 64-72. Also *Foundations*, Vol. X, pp. 19-35.

JOHN FOSTER (1770-1843) *1791

Entered College from Hebden Bridge, Yorkshire in 1791. Minister at Downend, Bristol. More celebrated as a writer.

J. E. Ryland: *Life and Correspondence of John Foster* (1846).

John Foster White: 'John Foster the Essayist', a lecture to the Halifax Antiquarian Society (1965), pp. 71-86. *D.N.B.* Vol. VII, p. 497; 'Memoir' in *B.M.* 1844, p. 1, 1846, p. 405.

[38] JAMES HINTON (1761-1823) *1784

John Howard Hinton: *Biographical Portraiture of James Hinton* (1824), p. 310.

[39] DR. JOHN RYLAND (1753-1825)

Son of John Collett Ryland.[13] Was born at Warwick, educated at his father's school at Northampton. In 1780 he married Elizabeth Tyler, who died in 1787. Two years later he married Francis Barrett who survived him. They had three daughters and one son, Jonathan Edward Ryland, who became secretary of the College, 1823-1825.

J. E. Ryland (his son), wrote a memoir, and list of his publications in *Pastoral Memorials* (1826), Vol. I, pp. 1-63.

James Culross: *The Three Rylands* (1897).

Robert Hall: *Sermon on the death of Reverend J. Ryland* (1825). R. Hall's *Works* (1832), Vol. I, pp. 371-414. *Baptist Magazine*, 1826, pp. 1-9. Obituary and List of his publications. *D.N.B.* XVII, p. 544.

F. A. Cox: *History of the B.M.S.* (1842), Vol. I, pp. 289-290.

L. G. Champion: 'The Theology of John Ryland, Its Sources and its Influences'. *B.Q.* XXVIII, January, 1979: 'The Letters of John Newton to John Ryland', *B.Q.* XXVII (1977), pp. 157-162.

[40] J. Ryland: *Advice to young ministers respecting their preparatory studies*, 1812.

[41] See letter in College Report 1812 and Appendix A.

[42] WILLIAM RHODES: *Baptist Magazine* 1833, p. 448.

[43] BENJAMIN DONNE, M.A. From 1789 until 1805 students had attended his philosophical lectures in Bristol. Then appointed by the College as 'Mathematics Tutor' (part time), and was remunerated 40 guineas per year by the Society until 1810.

THOMAS EXLEY, M.A. (1775-1855). Mathematics Tutor, 1810-1825. *D.N.B.* Vol. VI, p. 961.

[44] SUTCLIFF'S ACADEMY
Maurice F. Hewett (*1907): 'Sutcliff's Academy at Olney', *B.Q.* IV (1929), pp. 276-279; 'Sutcliff: The Meeting and the Man', unpublished MS. in College Library, pp. 115-120 gives details of the students of whom six came on to Bristol College.
Kenneth Howard: 'John Sutcliff of Olney', *B.Q.* XIV (1952), pp. 304-309.

[45] MICAH THOMAS AND HIS ACADEMY: see note 58.

[46] STOKES CROFT BUILDING
Swaine *op.cit.*, pp. 213-220 gives a detailed account.

[47] Robert Hall comments on 'the peculiar structures of Dr. Ryland's eyes which were a kind of natural microscope. The observations he made on various natural productions without the aid of instruments were really surprising; and though the peculiarity of his visual organs deprived him of the pleasure of contemplating the sublime and magnificent features of nature it gave him a singular advantage in tracing her minuter operations'.
Robert Hall's *Works* Vol. I (1832), p. 404.

[48] BAPTIST MISSIONARY SOCIETY
The College Annual Reports give some details of Bristol's contribution. For general surveys see:
F. A. Cox (*1798): *History of the Baptist Missionary Society, 1792-1842* (1842), 2 vols.
E. A. Payne: *The First Generation* (1936); *The Great Succession* (1938, 2nd ed. 1946); *South East from Serampore* (1945).

On Sierra Leone, Basil Amey: 'Baptist Missionary Society Radicals', *B.Q.* XXVI (1976), pp. 363-376.

On Jamaica, E. A. Payne: *Freedom in Jamaica* (1933, 2nd ed. 1946). W. F. Burchell: *Memoir of Thomas Burchell* (1849). G. A. Catherall (*1954): 'The Baptist Missionary Society and Jamaican Emancipation 1814-1845'. Unpublished thesis for M.A. Liverpool; and 'British Baptist Involvement in Jamaica 1783-1865', unpublished thesis for Ph.D., Keele (1971). 'Thomas Burchell: Gentle Rebel', *B.Q.* XXI (1966), pp. 349-363.

[49] BAPTIST UNION
    See E. A. Payne: *The Baptist Union: A Short History* (1959), pp. 15-27.

[50] J. G. FULLER: *Memoir of Reverend Thomas Roberts, M.A., and The History of King Street Church* (1842).

[51] ROBERT HALL (1764-1831)
    F. W. Trestrail: *Reminiscences of College Life in Bristol, during the ministry of Robert Hall 1825-1831*, p. 50. See *passim*.
    Gregory Olinthus: *Memoir* – Robert Hall's *Works*, Vol VI (1832), esp. p. 102.
    Graham Hughes: *Robert Hall* (1943).

[52] THOMAS STEFFE CRISP (1788-1868)
    Educated at Wymondley Academy (see McLachlan *op.cit.*, pp. 170-174) and at University of Glasgow.
    Minister of the Congregational Church, St. Ives 1809-1817.
    Tutor at Bristol 1818-1825. President 1825-1868.
    Dr. Edward Steane and Dr. F. W. Gotch. *Addresses at the funeral of T. S. Crisp* (1868).
    Swaine: *op.cit.*, pp. 335-342.
    F. W. Trestrail: *op.cit.*, pp. 21-23.

[53] WILLIAM ANDERSON (1784-1833) *1805. Minister at Dunstable 1810-1825. Classical Tutor at Bristol 1825-1833.
    Baptist Magazine 1833, pp. 445-492. F. W. Trestrail: *op.cit.*, pp. 23-30.

[54] DR. F. W. GOTCH (1808-1890), M.A., LL.D.
    Born in Kettering. Student at Bristol 1832-1834, at the Trinity College, University of Dublin 1834-1836, where he proceeded to a second rank moderatorship in Ethics. His course included Mathematics, Physics, Classics, Philosophy. Awarded B.A., M.A., and subsequently LL.D., degrees.

Minister at Boxmoor, Herts., 1836-1842.
Tutor in Philosophy and Natural Science at Stepney College
1842-1845. Tutor at Bristol 1845-1868. Resident Tutor 1861-
1868. President 1868-1883.
President of the Baptist Union 1868.
For Biography of F. W. Gotch see *Baptist Union Handbook* 1891,
p. 141, and *Northamptonshire Biographies* No. XVII (1901).
'The Gotch Family'.
Publications:
The Inspiration of the Holy Scriptures (1851); *Christ the Centre and
other papers* (1868); *Revised English Bible,* published by Eyre
and Spottiswoode (1877). Gotch was responsible for trans-
lating the Pentateuch.
A Supplement to Tischendorf's *Reliquiae ex Incendio Ereptae
Codicis Celeberrimi Cottoniani* (1881). The Cottonian MS. is
now in the British Museum. See Swaine, p. 360.

[55] For details of curriculum, see Annual Report for 1841.

[56] E. A. Payne: *The Baptist Union – A Short History* (1959), p. 72.

[57] STUDENTS of 1841 period

T. S. BAYNES
    E. J. Tongue: *Dr. Ward's Trust* (1951), pp. 39-40 (*B.Q.* XIII,
    1950, pp. 365-366). Swaine: pp. 267-270.

CHARLES STANFORD (1823-1886): *Memories and Letters* (1889),
    edited by his widow, pp. 241-242, lists of his 33 publications.
    D.N.B. XVIII, p. 886. *Baptist Union Handbook* 1887, p. 120.

EDWARD STEANE (1798-1882)
    Joint Secretary of the Baptist Union 1835-1882. President 1860.
    J. H. Hinton: *Life of James Hinton* (1824), pp. 241-250. *Baptist
    Union Handbook,* 1883, p. 276. E. A. Payne: *The Baptist Union*
    (1959).

GEORGE GOULD (1818-1882). President of Baptist Union 1879.
    Sermons and Addresses and Memoir by his son G. P. Gould (1883).

JOHN JENKYN BROWN (1808-1907). President of Baptist Union
    1882.
    Baptist Union Handbook, 1908, pp. 448-449.

JOHN TRAFFORD (1819-1890) *1837.
    Twelve Sermons with biographical notice by J. J. Brown (1892).
    Baptist Union Handbook, 1891 pp. 155-157.

RICHARD WEBLEY (1823-1869) (*1843).
    Baptist Union Handbook, 1870, p. 206.

[58] Other Baptist Colleges

1. Horton. Founded 1804. Moved to Rawdon 1859, Manchester 1964.

   J. O. Barrett: *A Short History of Rawdon College* (1954).
   J. Haslam in *The Baptists of Yorkshire*, pp. 279-284.
   Thomas Steadman: *Memoir of William Steadman* (1838).

2. Manchester. Founded at Bury 1866. Rawdon and Manchester amalgamated to become Northern College, Manchester, in 1964.
   Manchester Baptist College 1866-1916 (1916).

3. Stepney. Founded 1810. Removed to Regent's Park, London, 1856, and to Oxford 1927.

   R. E. Cooper: *From Stepney to St. Giles, 1810-1960* (1960).
   E. A. Payne: The Development of Nonconformist Theological Education in the Nineteenth Century, in *Studies in History and Religion* (1942), Chapter XIV.

4. Pastors' College. Now Spurgeon's College, London.
   Founded 1856. Removed to Metropolitan Tabernacle 1861, and to South Norwood Hill 1923.

   A. E. Wilmott: *Greater Things: a Popular History of Spurgeon's College*, London, 1968.
   G. H. Pike: *The Life and Work of Charles Haddon Spurgeon*, London, 6 vols.

5. South Wales. Founded at Abergavenny 1807. Moved to Pontypool 1836 and to Cardiff 1893, where it was joined by Haverfordwest College in 1899.

   D. Mervyn Himbury: *South Wales Baptist College 1807-1957* (1957).
   J. Jenkyn Brown: 'Memoir to Micah Thomas', *Baptist Magazine*, 1854, p. 593.
   E. W. Price Evans: 'Reverend Micah Thomas of Abergavenny, 1778-1853', *B.Q.* XIV (1951), pp. 109-113.

6. North Wales. Founded at Llangollen 1862. Moved to Bangor 1892.

   T. M. Bassett: *The Welsh Baptists* (1977), pp. 125-126, 195-197, 345-349.

7. Scotland. Founded at Glasgow 1894. *The Baptist Theological College of Scotland 1894-1944* (1944).
   G. Yuille: *History of Baptists in Scotland* (1926), pp. 250-259.

8. Midland Baptist College.
   A. C. Carter: *Midland Baptist College* (1925).

For details of discussions on Colleges and the Baptist Union,
see *The Baptist Record* 1846, pp. 357-391.
E. A. Payne: *The Baptist Union: A Short History* (1959).

[59] DR. JAMES C. CULROSS, M.A., D.D. (1824-1899)
Minister at Stirling 1850-1870; Highbury Hill, London, 1870-
1878; Adelaide Place, Glasgow, 1878-1883.
Principal, Bristol College, 1883-1896.
For his biography see: *Baptist Union Handbook*, 1900, p. 209.
G. Yuille: *History of Baptists in Scotland* (1926), pp. 250-255,
298.
J. C. Carlile: *The Story of English Baptists* (1905), pp. 260-261.
His addresses to the Baptist Union Assemblies of 1887-1888 are
printed in *Baptist Union Handbook* 1888, pp. 17-45.
Dr. Culross published about twenty-five books, mostly on
devotional and missionary topics.

[60] THE DOWN GRADE CONTROVERSY (1887-1888)
MS. correspondence between J. C. Culross and C. H. Spurgeon
November/December 1887 in College Library. See also E. A.
Payne: *Baptist Union*, pp. 127-143.

[61] UNIVERSITY COLLEGE – see note 71.

[62] BAPTIST MISSIONARY SOCIETY
Some of this detail is to be found only in the College Reports.
H. L. Hemmens: *George Grenfell: Pioneer in Congo* (1927), and
B.Q. XIII, July 1947, pp. 125-132;
Geo. Hawker (*1873): *George Grenfell* (1909), *D.N.B. Supple-
ment*, Vol. II, pp. 164-165.
H. R. Williamson *1904: *British Baptists in China, 1845-1952*
(1957).
E. W. Burt *1886: *After Sixty Years* (1937).

[63] S. A. SWAINE *1869
Faithful Men relates the history of the College until the
death of T. S. Crisp (1868).

[64] Henry Cook: *Charles Brown* (1939).

[65] BRISTOL BAPTIST ITINERANT SOCIETY founded 1824.
Sir John Swaish: *One hundred years of Village Preaching by the
Bristol Baptist Itinerant Society* (1924).
A. Gordon Hamlin: 'The Bristol Baptist Itinerant Society',
B.Q. Vol. XXI, pp. 321-324 (1966).
R. Whitehouse: *The Widening Circle* (1974).

[66] DR. WILLIAM JAMES HENDERSON (1843-1929).

Educated at Rawdon College. Minister at Bond Street, Birmingham, 1868-1873. Coventry, 1873-1894. Graduated B.A.(London), Hon. LL.D.(Bristol).

Joint President Bristol Baptist College, 1894-1896.

President, 1896-1923.

President of Baptist Union, 1907.

Memoirs. R. B. Henderson his son, headmaster of Alleyn's School, Dulverton, funeral address 5th May, 1929. Geo. Hawker: *Records and Reminiscences* (1922), pp. 17-20. *The Common Room* (1929), pp. 52-56; a magazine published by the students in the years 1926-1932 includes tributes by Dr. Dakin and former students.

[67] E. A. Payne: *The Free Church Tradition in the Life of England* (1944), p. 121.

[68] LECKIE ROBINSON FUND

Capital of £3,000 was donated by William Leckie Robinson, J.P., of Coventry to establish a fund 'to sustain one student every year while he is gaining experience as assistant of a minister who is in charge of some prosperous church' and/or 'to pay the fees of a lecturer or lecturers to deliver a course of lectures to the College'. Churches which received students for a year were Cardiff, High Wycombe, Ipswich, Manchester, Oxford, Portsmouth, Sheffield, Swindon, Watford – and Coventry.

[69] DR. H. H. ROWLEY (1890-1969), M.A., D.D., LL.D., B.Litt., F.B.A. *1910

From Melbourne Hall, Leicester. Minister at Wells, 1917-1922.

B.M.S. China, 1922-1930, including Tutor of Shantung Christian University, 1924-1929.

Assistant Lecturer, Cardiff University College, 1930-1934; Professor of Semitic Languages at University of Wales, Bangor, 1935-1945; Professor of Semitic Languages and Literature, Manchester University, 1945-1949; Professor of Hebrew Language and Literature, Manchester University, 1949-1959.

He received Hon. D.D., at Oxford in 1957 – the first Baptist so to be honoured.

President of the Baptist Union 1957.

M. Noth and D. Winton Thomas: *Wisdom in Israel and in the Ancient Near East* (1955): A *Festschift* presented to Dr. Rowley by the Society for Old Testament Study. Contains a bibliography of his numerous writings.
Memoir: *Baptist Handbook*, 1971, p. 391.

[70] WESTERN COLLEGE. See note 16.

[71] UNIVERSITY OF BRISTOL
1876 University College, Bristol, constituted as a School of Science and Literature for the West and South West of England and South Wales.
1893 The Bristol Medical School (founded 1832) incorporated into the University College as its Faculty of Medicine.
1909 Charter granted to University of Bristol. It incorporated the Merchant Venturers' College, which provided the Faculty of Engineering.
University and Community. Essays to mark the centenary of the founding of University College, Bristol (1976).

[72] *Edward Robinson, J.P.* by H. L. Taylor (1942).
DR. RICHARD GLOVER: Tribute by Dr. Charles Brown in College Annual Report, 1919.

[73] DR. C. D. WHITTAKER, M.A., LL.B.(Cantab), B.A., B.Sc., London (d. 1924).
Headmaster of Taunton School, 1899-1922.
S. P. Record, *Proud Century* (1948).

[74] DR. ARTHUR DAKIN (1884-1969), B.D.(London), D.Th.(Heidelberg).
Minister at Waterbarn, Lancs., 1910 – 14; Queen's Road, Coventry, 1914-1919; Ferme Park, London, 1919-1924; President Bristol College, 1924-1953; Principal Emeritus, 1953-1969.
President, Baptist Union, 1945.
W. W. Bottoms (*1927): 'Herald of God' in *The Communication of the Christian Faith*, ed. L. G. Champion (1964), pp. vii-xiv (see note 78).

[75] FRANK EDWARD ROBINSON (1859-1947); M.A.(Bristol), B.D. (London) *1884.
Tutor Bristol College, 1896-1937.
Memoir: *Baptist Union Handbook*, 1949.

[76] DR. G. HENTON DAVIES, M.A.(Wales), B.D.(Wales), B.Litt. (Oxon), D.D.(Glasgow).

Minister Hammersmith, London, 1935-1938; Tutor Bristol College, 1938-1951; Professor of Old Testament Studies, University of Durham, 1951-1958; Principal Regent's Park College, Oxford, 1958-1972. Principal Emeritus since 1972.

J. I. Durham and J. R. Porter: *Proclamation and Presence* (1970): *Old Testament essays in honour of Gwynne Henton Davies*.

Contains a biographical appreciation and bibliography of his writings.

[77] LAY TRAINING

For list of those awarded the certificate see College Report, 1952.

[78] *The Communication of the Christian Faith*, edited by Dr. L. G. Champion (1964). Presented to Dr. A. Dakin on the occasion of his 80th birthday, 21st November, 1964.

[79] DR. LEONARD G. CHAMPION, B.A.(Bristol), B.D.(London), D.Th. (Heidelberg). *1926.

Minister at Minehead, 1934-1938; Rugby, 1938-1953.

Tutor Bristol Baptist College, 1951-1953. President, 1953-1972. Principal Emeritus, 1972- .

President of the Baptist Union, 1964.

Moderator, National Free Church Federal Council, 1971.

[80] See Appendix C.

[81] Syllabus of B.A., in Theology. See College Annual Report, 1966.

[82] Churches which were served by student pastors between 1953 and 1978

By teams –
*Upper Studley, Shrewton, *Painswick, *Sharpness, Cheltenham (*Gas Green).

By student pastors –
*Bath, Hay Hill: *Oldfield Park, *Twerton; Bristol: Hotwells, *Little Stoke, Stapleton and Stoke Gifford; *Radstock, *Corsham.

*These churches are now supporting full-time ministers, or are grouped under a ministry.

Currently being served by student pastors under the supervision of staff.
Paulton (Somerset)
Bristol: Pill, Hillfields Park, Knowle West, Lawrence Weston, Stockwood and Cairns Road.

[83] DR. W. MORRIS S. WEST, M.A., D.Th., J.P.
Tutor Regent's Park College, 1953-1959. Minister at Dagnall Street, St. Albans, 1959-1971.
President Bristol College since 1972.
President-elect of the Baptist Union for 1979.

[84] STUDENTS
Of all the students who entered College since the open option policy began in 1969 and have now left, 55 (75%) have become ministers in Britain or are serving the Church overseas; 7 (10%) have married our students, and are serving with their husbands; 11 (15%) have entered other professions.

[85] LAY TRAINING
'A Conversation about Hope': *Study Encounter*, Vol. XI (1975), pp. 10-19 (World Council of Churches).

[86] REV. NEVILLE CLARK, M.A.(Oxon), S.T.M.
Educated Regent's Park College, M.A.(Oxon) and Union Theological Seminary, New York, S.T.M.
Assistant Secretary S.C.M., 1954-1956. Minister at Rochester, 1956-1959. Amersham, 1959-1975.
Tutor South Wales Baptist College and Lecturer at University College of South Wales since 1975.

[87] COLLEGE COMMUNITY 1978
37 students in College for the session 1978-1979 (entered 1974-1978). 27 men, 10 women; 26 single on entry, 11 married on entry; 14 under 21 years of age; 11 aged 21-25; 7 aged 26-34; 5 over 35.

[88] *In Deeper Waters* (1978) by Nick Fawcett, Martin North and John Elliston.

APPENDIX A

THE CASE FOR AN EDUCATED MINISTRY
BRISTOL EDUCATION SOCIETY 1770

INTRODUCTION

'The importance of a liberal education, more especially to candidates for the Christian ministry, is so exceedingly obvious, that one might almost think it impossible that any considerate, intelligent person should not be convinced of it. Yet there are, it is well known, some very worthy people who, from a mistaken view of things, not only call in question the importance of such an education, but even seem to imagine it is rather prejudicial than useful. Now, if these prejudices are well founded, every scheme formed for the education of pious youths designed for the ministry ought to be discountenanced. But if, on the other hand, it should appear that these prejudices are unreasonable, and that a learned education is highly useful, then every institution calculated for that purpose must be deserving of the warmest and most effectual encouragement. It is proposed, therefore, as introductory to an account of the BRISTOL EDUCATION SOCIETY, to offer a few thoughts on the usefulness and importance of learning to a Gospel minister; and, likewise, to lay down the plan of instruction at present pursued in that particular seminary, which it is the more immediate design of this Society to countenance and support.

'That all the learning in the world is, of itself, by no means sufficient to complete the ministerial character is readily acknowledged; and it is, therefore, a very great absurdity to think of training up young persons to the Christian ministry in the same indiscriminate manner as to any other profession. If a man be not truly religious, and furnished with talents adapted to the work of the ministry, let him have as much learning as may be, it cannot be expected that he should be an acceptable and useful minister. And it is much to be apprehended that an abuse of learning, in this respect, hath contributed more than anything to bring it into disrepute. Let it, therefore, be remembered, all that is pleaded for in this introduction, is the usefulness and importance of learning in *subordination* to what is more essentially requisite to the ministerial character. Many persons without any of the advantages of learning, we freely confess, have been very able, laborious, and successful ministers of the Gospel. But not a few of these ministers themselves, so far from decrying learning as useless, have sensibly felt their own want of it, and with an amiable candor acknowledged the disadvantages they lay under on that account. And, indeed, it is highly unreasonable, as well as ungrateful, for those who are destitute of learning, to exclaim against it, since they are not to be supposed very competent judges of the matter, and are themselves under peculiar obligations to the WORKS of the learned. The expressions of an eminent divine upon this subject, in a late important publication, are remarkably strong: "Here I cannot but observe the amazing ignorance and stupidity of some persons who take it into their heads to decry learning and learned men. For what would they have done for a Bible if it had not been for them as instruments? And if they had it, so as to have been capable of reading it, God must have wrought a miracle for them, and continued that miracle in every nation, in every age, and to every individual; I mean the gift of tongues in a supernatural way, as was bestowed upon the Apostles on the Day of Pentecost; which there is no reason in the world ever to have expected. Bless God, therefore, and be thankful that God has, in His Providence, raised up such men to translate the Bible into the mother tongue of every nation, and particularly into ours; and that He still continues to raise up such, who are able to defend the translation made against erroneous persons and enemies of the truth; and to correct and amend it in lesser matters in which it may have failed, and clear and illustrate it by their learned notes upon it."

'It has been suggested by some that LEARNING is designed to perfect the work of the Spirit of God. But this is a mere slander. The only question is, Are we to expect miracles, as in the Apostolic age, to qualify us for the work of the ministry; or, are we to use ordinary means? That we are not to expect miracles all will allow, and, if not, then surely we are to use ordinary means. And so far is this from interfering with the work of the Spirit, that it appears to be the only way in which we may reasonably expect His continued influences; and it seems rather to be tempting the Spirit of God to expect that in an *extraordinary*, which we are authorised to expect only in an *ordinary* way. We have already observed that no man can be an acceptable minister of the Gospel if he be not a converted man, and furnished with those ministerial gifts or talents which God alone can communicate; but, then, is he not to endeavour, in the use of proper means, to improve these talents? Suppose a man who is not able to read should yet appear to be an eminently good man, and to have such a peculiar readiness in expressing his sentiments, both in prayer and religious conference, as should lead a Christian society to judge he might be useful in the work of the ministry; must not this man be taught to read lest it should be supposed to interfere with the work of the Spirit of God? Or, if he is taught to read the Scriptures in the languages in which they were written, that he may be able the better to enter into the genuine spirit and meaning of the sacred writers, and judge for himself the propriety and force of any Scripture criticism; if he is taught the rules of just reasoning, and how to arrange his ideas in the most clear and orderly manner; if he is led into the knowledge of ancient customs, and the history of past ages, by which he may be enabled to elucidate many passages of Scripture; if he be made acquainted with the rudiments of natural philosophy, by which his ideas of the Divine perfections and the work of God may be enlarged and elevated; in short, if he be led through such a course of instruction as hath a natural tendency, with the blessing of God, to enable him to exercise his ministerial talents with more general acceptance and usefulness, what injury is done to him? Or, what reflection, can it be pretended, is hereby cast upon the work of the Spirit of God? Is it lawful for a person who may be called to the ministry, to learn to read, if he was not before capable of it? Is it lawful for him to avail himself of a learned exposition or commentary? Is it lawful for him to premeditate what he intends to say upon any subject, and seek out acceptable words? And is it *unlawful*, then, to proceed one step further? Must we stop *precisely* here? Or, may we not learn the languages in which the Scriptures were written, with other things of a similar nature? The opposers of learning, to be consistent with themselves, should neither read nor study at all, since, upon their principles, they are hereby attempting to help or mend the work of the Spirit of God.

'The truth is, whatever prejudices may be formed in the minds of some men against learning, it is certain that since the times of the Apostles, who had those miraculous helps which superseded every kind of learning, Divine Providence hath, in every age, put the greatest honour upon it. Consult the history of the Church, and you will uniformly find through every period of it, with *very few* exceptions, that those ministers who have been the most laborious and success-ful in their work, have been as eminent for sound learning as for substantial piety. Nor is it to be doubted but that, whenever there is a revival of religion amongst us, men will be raised up, not only eminent for spiritual gifts, but who will endeavour zealously to improve those gifts, for the attainment of all that knowledge which, with the blessing of God, may render them able ministers of the New Testament. For though we have no sort of doubt but that the great Head of the Church could, if He pleased, carry on His work, not only without *learned* ministers but without *any* ministers at all; yet, as He sees fit, for the most part, to fulfil His designs in the use of means, it is in this way we are to expect His presence and blessing. There is, moreover, this further advantage arising from learning, it will enable a minister to become an instructor of youth, by which his sphere of usefulness may be enlarged, and he may be enabled to procure, with reputation, a subsistence for himself and family, in many situa-tions, where otherwise he could not.

'The Seminary countenanced by the Society, which now solicits the assistance of the friends of religion and learning, is at present under the direction of the Rev. *Hugh Evans*, assisted by the Rev. Messrs. *Caleb Evans*, and *James Newton*, who are ready chearfully to exert their united endeavours to accomplish, as humble instruments in the hands of Divine Providence, the pious intentions of the generous subscribers to this institution.'

BRISTOL'S APPEAL TO THE GENTLEMEN OF LONDON 1770

To the Gentlemen and other serious Christians in London, who have the cause of Christ, and the honour of the Christian Ministry at heart.

The office of the Christian Ministry, rightly understood, is the most honour-able and important, that any man in the whole world can ever sustain, and it will be one of the wonders and employments of eternity, to consider the reasons, why the wisdom and goodness of God assigned this office to imperfect and guilty man.

It is an office and character that is deeply interested in the highest concerns of God's glory and perfections. It is an employment that obliges a man to the closest attention, to find out the true mind of God in the Holy Scriptures. It is a work in which we are called, to instruct the minds of men in the noblest knowledge, and teach them to adore and love God. The great design and intention of the office of a Christian preacher, is, to restore the throne and dominion of God in the souls of men; to display in the most lively colours, and proclaim in the clearest language, the wonderful perfections, offices, and grace of the Son of God; and to attract the souls of men into a state of everlasting friendship with Him.

It is an office and work, the grand design of which is to turn the sons and daughters of Adam from darkness to light, from guilt to pardon, from corruption to holiness, and from ruin to eternal happiness. It is an employment, that, when finished with wisdom and faithfulness, will be crowned with higher honours than were ever bestowed on the best kings, the most renowned heroes, or most celebrated philosophers.

It is a work which an archangel might wish for, as an honour to his character;

yea, an office which every angel in heaven might covet to be employed in for a thousand years to come.

It is such an honourable, important, and useful office, that if a man is put into it by God, and made faithful and successful through life, he may look down with disdain upon a crown, and shed a tear of pity on the brightest monarch on earth.

It is a work, that, when a man is called to it by the providence and grace of God, should be entered upon with fear and trembling. It should be approached with a mixture of terror and joy, of awful reverence, and holy pleasure. No man should dare to rush into it, uncalled by God, or unqualified by the gifts and graces of the Holy Spirit.

There is requisite to this office, an enlightened mind, a renewed heart, very tender affections, a fervent love to the souls of men; a fixed attention to, and delight in, the holy Scriptures, and a peculiar love to Christ; an ability to speak in proper instructive words; a firmness of mind, to resist all opposition; and the utmost care to preserve a good moral character in the Church and the world.

To all the above qualifications, it is necessary and important, that young men, before they enter upon the full work of it, should have a very considerable length of time to be separated from all the business and cares of the world, and in a great measure from the conversation and company of most Christians too; in order to acquire a habit of thinking closely; to exercise themselves in contemplation and prayer; to converse much with God, and their own hearts; to study the sacred Scriptures in the original languages, with the utmost diligence and attention; and, especially, to improve by them in a way of devotional exercise.

For want of this useful and necessary preparation, many young men, of promising gifts, have been pushed too soon into public and started work. And what has been the consequence? The churches know the consequence; but the young persons themselves have most severely felt the fruits of the hasty proceedings. They have, to their cost and pungent sorrow, been sufferers for many years.

On the other hand, there may be an extreme likewise; not in the length of time allotted for preparatory studies, but in the misapplication of that time; or wasting too much of it in studies, that have no tendency to form a solid and judicious ministry of the Gospel.

Certainly every thing should be made subservient to Divinity; and the best hours of every day, from the first moment to the last, should be employed in gaining, by close attention and prayer, a masterly knowledge of all the great doctrines of the Gospel, and the richest methods of improving them in a practical and devotional manner. And if this is done to purpose, be assured, Sirs, there will be no time for trifling, in the space of four, five or six years. This is the highest work, and the noblest employment of a young student. And if he has the strong, and capacious mind of an Owen, a Charnock, or a Witsius, he will find full work for it, not only in the course of his studies, but all the days of his life.

The scarcity of serious and evangelical ministers of our denomination, has been long complained. If the Lord should remove a few of our aged and useful fathers, their loss will be most severely felt. The places of good and faithful servants of God are not soon filled up; an able minister of the New Testament is not formed in a day or a year, no, nor in seven or ten years; happy is that young man, who arrives to any degree of maturity, and strength of mind, in the compass of twenty years! I am sure it is worth twenty years study to be able to state clearly, and defend and improve the truths of our holy religion. I dare affirm, that I have the concurring sentiments of all those, who are best able to judge in this matter.

If these things are true, then how careful and zealous ought we to be, to encourage and assist all young men in our churches, who appear to be endued, not only with grace, but gifts for the ministry; or shall we sit still and say, 'The Lord Jesus will provide, by a miracle, for all the wants of His people and churches, and there is no need to use any means at all?' But, my friends, does He do so in providence for your bodies and families? Did He give you all your wealth, and trade, and spacious houses, by a miracle?

Does He act thus in His dispensations of grace, in order to your growth in knowledge, and holiness, and the comforts of religion? Are you not obliged to use diligently all the means of grace, and constantly too, in order to have the comforts of grace?

Now ought serious Christians to use time and pains to grow in knowledge and grace; and have not ministers, who are to preach the great truths of God every week to hundreds of immortal souls, have they not need of all possible assistance from heaven and earth? And can we have the heart to refuse them any encouragement in our power, especially in their preparations for this glorious work? No; my honoured Friends and Gentlemen, let us no longer lie in a state of indifference and disunion; but let us all, to a man, join our hearts, our purses, and our prayers, in this dearest and best of all causes; and, instead of starting frivolous objections, to diminish or cool the generous dispositions of any, let us rather fan the fire into a brighter flame, and love those persons best who are the most able and ready to promote so good a work!

Till the great Head of the Church shall be pleased to excite some abler hand to lay better proposals before you, please to accept of the following considerations:
1. Our honoured and dear brethren, of our denomination in Bristol, being animated by a truly laudable and public spirit, are now entering upon more vigorous methods, to provide for the education of the young men, who may be placed under their care; and are inviting you to concur with them in a general subscription, to raise a fund for this purpose.
2. This matter is of such great and extensive concern, that there can be no excuses or reason for any man to withhold his assistance; because all will be little enough to carry on such a glorious design.
3. As you will doubtless judge it reasonable and kind to concur with the views of the Bristol Society, and give them ample assistance; it is humbly proposed to consideration, whether you would direct all your strength to that department of our Redeemer's interest, or would choose to reserve a small portion of your annual supplies to any other quarter nearer London. If the latter is chosen, as will probably be the case,
4. It is then humbly proposed to look out amongst our elder ministers of the Gospel within a day's journey of London, and see if we cannot find a man, who is disengaged from the cares of a numerous family, unencumbered with any Boarding-School for boys; and who has, by his years and studies, attained the general esteem of the ministers and churches of London, and who will readily undertake the care of five or six pupils only, in order to train them up in the solid knowledge of all the parts of divinity.
5. That a trial shall be made for one year, under such regulations as the sub-scribers shall think proper: And at the end of the first year, the pupils shall be subject to the examination of the London Ministers and Gentlemen, with respect to their good behaviour, and their improvement in a manly knowledge of the Holy Scriptures.

6. That if upon trial it shall appear, that the tutor and pupils have done their duty, a second year shall be allowed; and then a third and a fourth, as shall seem good upon the wisest deliberation; And with such farther rules for their studies, as shall be thought best to encourage and forward the grand design of the whole, viz. the glory of Christ, and the regular provision for the wants of the churches in this part of the Kingdom

ACADEMIC STUDIES

The following extracts from the Annual Reports of the Bristol Education Society in Dr. Ryland's time indicate concern for improvement in the Baptist Denomination:

'Without an understanding of the languages in which the Scriptures were originally written, acquaintance with the various branches of science which enlarge the mind and are rendered subservient to the diffusion of scriptural knowledge, our ministers must appear inferior to those of other denominations: while they will be less able to defend the great truths of our holy religion against infidels and the patrons of error; or to vindicate our views of those secondary points in which we are constrained to differ from our fellow Christians' (1804).

It was recognised that applicants varied in their educational background and capacities. In an attempt to meet this situation, the Society often placed students under 'a respectable minister' for a preparatory year. As many as six were in this situation in 1807, some under John Sutcliff at Olney, others at Birmingham and Leominster. Such students are described as 'having received very little education in their earlier years, or possessing little genius for learning, are unable to apply with advantage to the study of languages, and yet would be capable of such improvement as would render them serviceable in the work of the ministry to congregations in more retired situations'.

'Your Committee cannot refrain from expressing their conviction that the circumstances of the times demand greater attention than ever to the education of persons designed for the ministerial office. And in this education, let it be understood, they consider that biblical and theological knowledge should ever hold the first place. One of the most important advantages of the Christian ministry, considered as a separate occupation, is that by allowing time for study and reflection, a more profound and extensive knowledge of the truths of revelation may be acquired than it is possible for those persons to attain, whose lives are spent in secular employments.

'Should there be any persons in our connexion, who are not yet fully sensible of the importance of rendering the education of our ministers proportionate to the general standard of information, or who may be apprehensive that studious habits are incompatible with Christian zeal, they may be reminded of one obvious fact in ecclesiastical history, that the men most distinguished for zeal in the cause of true religion, that the greatest reformers, the most intrepid martyrs, the most zealous missionaries, have been men of extensive knowledge and erudition. Such were Luther, Calvin, and Melancthon; such, in our own Island, were Wickliff, Knox, and Melville; such were those worthies, the New England settlers, one of whose first measures after they had obtained a refuge from persecution, was to found a college for their ministerial candidates; such were Elliott, Schwartz, and Martyn' (1823).

A Sub-Committee was set up to consider ways in which the teaching and organisation of the College could be improved. The recommendations are contained in the 1825 Report.

THE GIFFORD COLLECTION

SOME OF THE BIBLES, MANUSCRIPTS AND OTHER EARLY BOOKS ON DISPLAY AT THE COLLEGE

ENGLISH VERSION OF THE BIBLE

Wycliffe	New Testament Epistles, including the Epistle to the Laodiceans, Acts of Apostles and the Apocalypse. John Wycliff's translation. Manuscript on vellum. 14th century.		
Tyndale	New Testament	1526	Printed at Worms by Peter Shoeffer. One of only two copies known to survive; the other copy in St. Paul's Cathedral, is very imperfect. Facsimile by Francis Fry 1867; Facsimile by Paradine. 1976.
	Pentateuch	1534	
	New Testament	1548	With the Epistles of the Old Testament.
		1549	With Erasmus's exhortation.
		1552	With an address to King Edward VI.
		1553	With Epistles of the Old Testament.
Coverdale	Bible	1537	
	Bible	1550	
Taverner	Bible	1539	
Cranmer	Bible	1539	(The Great Bible.)
	Bible	1540	(Third Edition) with Preface by Archbishop Cranmer.
Matthews	Bible	1549	Revised by Edmunde Becke.
		1551	With Sternhold and Hopkins' Psalms (1565-1570).
Whittingham	New Testament	1557	
Genevan	Bible	1560	First Edition
	Bible	1562	
Bishops'	Bible	1568	
		1575	With Sternhold and Hopkins' Psalms.
Tomson's Revision of Genevan version			
	New Testament	1596	
Rheims	New Testament	1582	First Edition, with table of controversies.
Douay	Bible	1609-1610 (2 vols)	
			Old Testament and Apocrypha.
Authorised Version			
	Bible	1611	First edition. The 'He' Bible. So called because of the wrong reading at Ruth 3:15.
	Bible	1611	First edition. The 'She' Bible. With the correct reading in Ruth.
	Bible	1612	Quarto. With Speed's Genealogies.

MEDIEVAL MANUSCRIPTS

Latin Vulgates
    Biblia Sacra and Apocrypha: with prologue of Jerome.
        Illuminated manuscript on vellum. 13th
        century
    Biblia Sacra and Apocrypha: with prologue.
        Manuscript on vellum, with illuminated
        initial letters. 13th century.

An Ancient Chronicle – Historia Britonum.
        Manuscript on vellum with illuminated initial
        letters. 14th century.

Paris Book of Hours   Manuscript on vellum, with decorative
        illuminated margins. 15th century.

Private Devotions   Preces Privatae Catholicae, partly in English.
        Manuscript on vellum. 15th century.

Processional   Processionale with musical notes, formerly
        belonging to the Monastery of S. Salvatoris
        et S. Brigitte de Syon.

Breviary   Officium Beatae Mariae Virginis. 15th
        century manuscript used by Franciscan nuns.

OTHER EARLY PRINTED WORKS

Latin Vulgates Biblia Sacra   Printed in Cologne, 1479.
        Biblia Latina   Printed by C. Froschoour, Zurich 1543.

Greek New Testament   Novum Testamentum Graece with Latin
        translation by Erasmus, 1522.

Primer   In English and Latin set forth by King
        Edward VI, 1546. 8vo.

Tyndale, Frith and Barnes   Works: with preface by John Foxe, 1573.

Fulke's Confution of the Rhemish New Testament, 1589
        With Rheims and Bishops' Versions in
        Parallel.

Concordances to the Bible by J. Marbek, 1550
        Another begun by Vavasour Powell, and
        enlarged.
        John Bunyan's copy with his autograph, 1673.

Foxe's Book of Martyrs   An early example of a chained book.
        16th century.

APPENDIX C

SECRETARIES AND TREASURERS OF THE COLLEGE

Secretaries

1770-1778	Thomas Mullett
1779-1790	Dr. Caleb Evans
1791-1792	James Norton
1792-1799	John Hughes
1799-1802	Joseph Dear
1802-1816	Rev. Henry Page
1817	Rev. Thomas Roberts
1817-1823	Andrew Livett
1823-1825	John E. Ryland
1826-1833	J. G. Fuller
1833-1841	Joseph Ash
1841-1863	George C. Ashmead
1863-1871	Rev. N. Haycroft
1871-1873	Rev. R. P. MacMaster
1873-1919	Dr. Richard Glover
1919-1922	Rev. F. G. Benskin (co-Sec.)
1919-1947	Rev. Chas. Brown (Hon.)
1922-1925 1934-1946	Rev. R. C. Griffin (co-Sec.)
1925-1934	Rev. Horace D. Hilliard
1946-1960	Dr. Edwin J. Tongue
1960-1965	Rev. Raymond P. Taylor
1965-1975	Rev. Geo. W. Byrt
1975-	Rev. C. Sidney Hall

Treasurers

1770-1783	John Bull
1784-1788	Francis Bull
1789-1812	John Page
1812-1822	Edward Daniell
1823-1825	Joseph Sherring
1826-1838	Isaac Leonard
1838-1863	Robert Leonard
1863-1867	Joseph Eyre
1867-1885	Elisha S. Robinson
1885-1935	Edward Robinson
1935-1951	Harry L. Taylor
1951-1954	Harold W. Bodey
1954-1975	Harold W. Eyles
1975-	Raymond W. Montacute

APPENDIX D

PRESIDENTS OF THE BAPTIST UNION
who were students or staff at Bristol College

1833	Rev. Dr. John Rippon
1834	Rev. Dr. F. A. Cox (also 1845 and 1852)
1836	Rev. C. E. Birt
1837	Rev. John H. Hinton (also 1863)
1839	Rev. Thomas Swan
1840	Rev. James Acworth (also 1856, 1859 and 1861)
1841	Rev. James Sprigg
1844	Rev. Robert Roff
1846	Rev. John E. Giles
1851	Rev. James Hoby (also 1854)
1860	Rev. Edward Steane
1864	Rev. James P. Mursell
1868	Rev. Dr. Frederick W. Gotch
1870	Rev. William Robinson
1877	Rev. John T. Brown
1879	Rev. George Gould
1880	Rev. Frederick Trestrail
1882	Rev. J. Jenkyn Brown
1887	Rev. Dr. James Culross
1890	Rev. James Owen
1892	Rev. Robert H. Roberts
1898	Rev. Samuel Vincent
1907	Rev. Dr. W. J. Henderson
1908	Rev. Dr. Charles Brown
1945	Rev. Dr. Arthur Dakin
1951	Rev. Dr. H. R. Williamson
1957	Rev. Dr. H. H. Rowley
1962	Rev. W. D. Jackson
1964	Rev. Dr. Leonard G. Champion
1971	Rev. Dr. G. Henton Davies
1973	Rev. Douglas H. Hicks
1979	Rev. Dr. W. M. S. West

SECRETARIES OF THE BAPTIST UNION

1813-1819	Rev. Thomas Thomas
1835-1882	Rev. Edward Steane
1841-1866	Rev. John Howard Hinton
1880-1882	Rev. William Sampson

CHAIRMEN OF THE BAPTIST MISSIONARY SOCIETY

1922-1924	Rev. Dr. Charles Brown
1955-1956	Rev. Dr. H. R. Williamson
1959-1960 1961-1962	Rev. Dr. H. H. Rowley
1977-1978	Rev. E. G. T. Madge
1978-1979	Rev. W. Murray Raw

SECRETARIES OF THE BAPTIST MISSIONARY SOCIETY

1815-1817	The Reverend James Hinton
1815-1825	The Reverend Dr. John Ryland
1849-1869	The Reverend Dr. Frederick Trestrail
1879-1912	The Reverend J. B. Myers
1939-1951	The Reverend Dr. H. R. Williamson
1959-1976	The Reverend E. G. T. Madge

APPENDIX E

PRINCIPALS AND TUTORS

Principals[1]

1720-1758	Rev. Bernard Foskett
1758-1781	Rev. Hugh Evans, M.A.
1781-1791	Rev. Caleb Evans, D.D.
1793-1825	Rev. John Ryland, D.D.
1825-1868	Rev. Thomas S. Crisp
1868-1883	Rev. Frederick W. Gotch, M.A., LL.D.
1883-1896	Rev. James C. Culross, M.A., D.D.
1894-1922	Rev. William J. Henderson, B.A., LL.D.[2]
1922-1924	Rev. Charles D. Whittaker, M.A., LL.D., B.Sc.
1924-1953	Rev. Arthur Dakin, B.D., D.Th.
1953-1972	Rev. Leonard G. Champion, B.A., B.D., D.Th.
1972-	Rev. W. Morris S. West, M.A., D.Th.[3]

Tutors

1728-1729	Rev. Andrew Gifford, D.D.
1733-1758	Rev. Hugh Evans
1758-1781	Rev. Caleb Evans, D.D.
1770-1790	Rev. James Newton, M.A.
1785-1791	Rev. Robert Hall, M.A.
1791-1796	Rev. Joseph Hughes, M.A.
1796-1825	Rev. Isaac James
1802-1817	Rev. Henry Page, M.A.
1818-1825	Rev. Thomas S. Crisp
1825-1833	Rev. William Anderson
1834-1845	Rev. Edgar Huxtable, M.A.
1845-1868	Rev. Frederick W. Gotch, M.A., LL.D.
1860-1867	Rev. Frank Bosworth, M.A.
1868-1872	Mr. E. W. Claypole, B.A., B.Sc.
1872-1878	Mr. Donald Bassett, B.A., LL.B.
1896-1937	Rev. Frank E. Robinson, M.A., B.D.
1937-1951	Rev. G. Henton Davies, M.A., B.D., B.Litt., D.D.
1951-1953	Rev. L. G. Champion, B.A., B.D., D.Th.
1953-	Rev. Norman S. Moon, B.A., M.Th.
1959-	Rev. Harry Mowvley, M.A.
1977-	Rev. Keith Clements, M.A.

Notes
1. Since 1770 the Principal has also been President of the Bristol Education Society.
2. Co-Principal with Dr. Culross 1894-1896.
3. Principal-elect 1971-1972. President since 1972.

Part-time tutors have not been included.

APPENDIX F

ACADEMIC OFFICES HELD BY FORMER STUDENTS

Rev. James Acworth, M.A., Ll.D.	President, Horton Academy and Rawdon College	1835-1863
Rev. Robert Aspland	Principal, Hackney Unitarian College	1813-1818
Dr. Thomas S. Baynes, Ll.D.	Professor of Logic, St. Andrews University	1867-1887
Rev. A. H. Bell, M.A., B.D.	Professor of Parkyn College, Adelaide	? -1955
Dr. G. H. Boobyer, B.A., B.D., D.Th.	Lecturer in Divinity, Newcastle, University of Durham	1948-1957
	Head of Department of Divinity, University of Newcastle	1957-1967
Rev. E. C. Burleigh, M.A., B.D.	Tutor, Baptist College, Melbourne	1944-1952
	Principal, South Australian Baptist College	1952-1969
Rev. E. W. Burt, M.A.	Dean, School of Theology, Shantung Christian University, China	1887-1933
Rev. Francis Clowes, M.A.	Tutor, Horton Academy	1836-1851
Rev. Francis A. Cox, M.A.	Tutor, Stepney College	1813-1822
Rev. Charles Daniell	Tutor, Horton Academy	1855-1859
Rev. Benjamin Davies, Ph.D., Ll.D.	President, Baptist College, Montreal	1838-1844
	President, Stepney College	1844-1847
	Professor, McGill University, Montreal	1847-1857
	Tutor, Regent's Park College, London	1857-1875
Rev. Gethyn Davies, B.A., D.D.	Tutor, North Wales Baptist College, Llangollen	1872-1883
	President, North Wales Baptist College, Bangor	1883-1896
Rev. Thomas Davies, D.D.	President, Haverfordwest College	1857-1894
Rev. David Davies, B.A., B.D.	Tutor, Calabar College, Jamaica	1911-1948
Rev. L. V. Dickins, B.A., B.D.	Tutor, Serampore College, India	1928-1929
Rev. Morgan Edwards, M.A.	Founder, Brown University, Rhode Island	1764
Rev. Rudolf E. Eksteins, B.A.	Tutor, Baptist Seminary, Riga, Latvia	1928-1939
Rev. John Evans, Ll.D., M.A.	Tutor, General Baptist Academy, London	1795-1818
Rev. Stephen Freeman	Tutor, General Baptist Academy, London	1792-1794
Rev. F. W. Gotch, M.A., Ll.D.	Tutor, Stepney College, London	1842-1845

Rev. Joshua Gray, Ph.D.	Tutor, Stepney College	1851-1854
Rev. Gwenyth Hubble, B.A., B.D.	Principal, Carey Hall, Birmingham	1945-1960
Rev. Forbes A. M. Jackson, M.A.	Principal, Harley College, London	1901-1910
Rev. Otto Koenig	Professor, Rochester Theological Seminary, U.S.A.	1921-1932
Rev. Mikko Kolomainen	Principal, Baptist Seminary, Finland	1949-
Rev. John Leechman, M.A., Ll.D.	Tutor, Serampore College, India	1832-1837
Rev. John Mack	Professor, then Principal Serampore College, India	1822-1845
Rev. Kenneth Manley, B.A., D.Phil.	Tutor, Baptist College, Adelaide	1969-1971
	Tutor, New South Wales Baptist College	1972-
Rev. Joshua Marshman, D.D.	Tutor, then Principal Serampore College, India	1818-1837
Rev. Ernest Price, B.A., B.D.	President, Calabar College, Jamaica	1910-1937
Rev. R. H. Roberts, B.A.	President, Regent's Park College, London	1893-1896
Rev. E. Roberts-Thomson, M.A., D.D.	Principal, New Zealand Baptist College	1953-1960
	Principal, New South Wales Baptist College, Australia	1961-1964
Rev. H. H. Rowley, M.A., D.D., B.Litt., F.B.A.	Tutor, Shantung Christian University, China	1924-1929
	Lecturer, Cardiff University College	1930-1934
	Professor, Semitic Languages, Bangor, North Wales	1935-1945
	Professor, Semitic Languages, Manchester	1945-1949
	Professor, Hebrew Languages and Literature, Manchester	1949-1959
Rev. William Sampson	Tutor, Serampore College, India	1860-1866
Rev. Charles Spurden, D.D.	President, Fredericton College, New Brunswick, Canada	1843-1867
Rev. Wm. Staughton, D.D.	Principal, Burlington Academy, U.S.A.	1798-1805
	President, Columbian University, U.S.A.	1822-1829
Rev. Wm. Steadman, D.D.	President, Horton Academy	1805-1835
Rev. Thomas Swan	Tutor, Serampore College, India	1825-1827
Rev. George Thomas, M.A.	Tutor, Pontypool	1841-1871
Rev. Joseph W. Thomas	Tutor, Serampore College, India	1867-1880
Rev. Micah Thomas	Principal, Abergavenny	1807-1836
Rev. Joshua Tinson	President, Calabar College, Jamaica	1843-1850
Rev. John Trafford, M.A.	Principal, Serampore College, India	1854-1879
Rev. Keith Tucker, M.A.	Principal, Calabar College, Jamaica	1948-1958

Rev. W. M. S. West, M.A., D.Th.	Tutor, Regent's Park College, Oxford	1953-1959
Rev. J. S. Whitewright	President, Gotch-Robinson Institution, China	1893-1921
Rev. William Yates, D.D.	Tutor, Serampore College, India	1815-1817
Rev. Solomon Young, M.A.	Tutor, Stepney College	1813-1827
	President	1827

In addition the following served Bristol College
As Principals: Hugh Evans, F. W. Gotch, L. G. Champion, W. M. S. West
As Tutors: Robert Hall, Isaac James, Henry Page, William Anderson,
              Frank Robinson, Norman Moon, Harry Mowvley
(see Appendix E)

AREAS FROM WHICH STUDENTS CAME

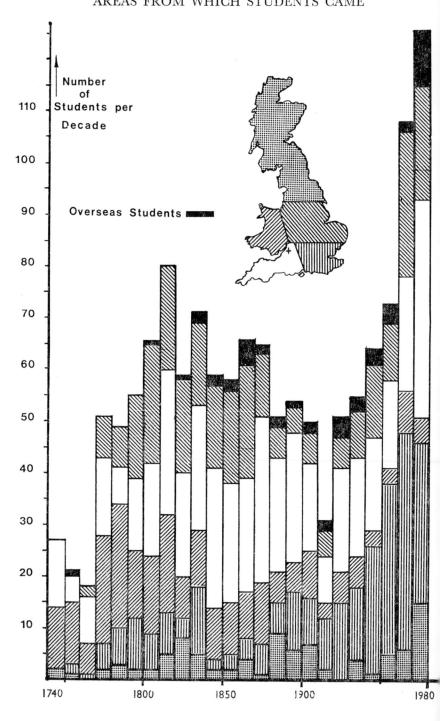

Number of Students per Decade

110

100

90   Overseas Students ▬

80

70

60

50

40

30

20

10

1740   1800   1850   1900   1980

THE COST OF EDUCATING MINISTERS

HOW IT HAS BEEN MET

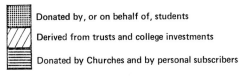

Donated by, or on behalf of, students

Derived from trusts and college investments

Donated by Churches and by personal subscribers

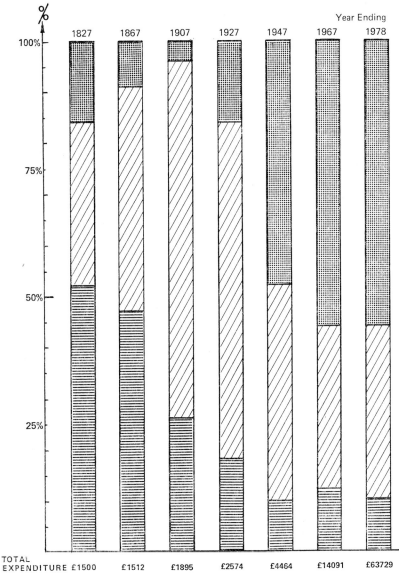

	1827	1867	1907	1927	1947	1967	1978
TOTAL EXPENDITURE	£1500	£1512	£1895	£2574	£4464	£14091	£63729
NUMBER OF STUDENTS	21	22	20	21	27	43	43

Index